BEETLE LOVE ♥

DELIUS KLASING VERLAG

First love. Like the crush on the girl or boy next door.

A love
that lasts
forever

I don't know how many school desks I drew this Beetle on. Front view. Tree to the left, fence to the right. Path. Meadow. I have to admit, a Beetle is pretty much the only thing I can draw. Apart from dot-to-dot pictures, maybe. There has always been a Beetle in my life, one way or the other. When I was born, my parents drove me home from the hospital in a "Marathon Metallic" Volkswagen Beetle 1303 LS. I survived two accidents in this car. In a chrome metal frame car seat that was equipped with a wooden tray (so the boy can play on long journeys) instead of a harness.

Beetles were everywhere. When I was old enough to drive a car myself, that was precisely the reason why I did not buy one.

Many of my friends drove Beetles. Preferably painted "Mint Green", lowered and souped up. In the late 1980s, the Californian crashed onto the European V-Dub scene like a wave. Especially France and England contributed many colourful conversions. I was fascinated by a rally in Menton on the Côte d'Azur, where I saw air cooled VWs that looked like I had never seen them looking before.

My first car was a turquoise VW 1600 TL; it was so unusual – and, unfortunately, also so rusty that I had to restore it with the help of a friend before I could drive it. I kept it for 25 years and two months and now drive a VW 1600 Notchback and a Squareback. The Type 3 is somehow just a bigger Beetle, after all.

Although I have to admit to a brief but passionate fling: with an Alpine White VW 1200 from Mexico, special edition "Jeans Bug". To be honest, I bought the car because I didn't want to drive the TL in the winter. However, I'll never forget my trips in this brave little Beetle.

Instagram 1973. **A click, a Kodak negative, a moment captured on camera. Eyes already on a Beetle at the beginning of a life-long passion.**

Like the day when I proudly overtook modern cars that were careering all over the place on the A45 motorway in driving snow thanks to my winter tyres, which were so rough that they effortlessly ploughed through the snow. Or the day when I drove it to the VW-Euro-Rally in Baarlo, or the drive to the Bug Show in Spa. "It" was actually a "she". Helga, because that was the name of her first owner.

I sold the Jeans Bug, saw it around from time to time. A close acquaintance took it, or rather her, off my hands. After a while, she sold the little car on as well, and we lost track of her. However, Beetle Love never dies. I now draw a Beetle, viewed from the front, more often again. Tree to the left, fence to the right.

Path. Meadow. My virtual garage with a major online used car sales platform is usually full of Beetles. One day, I'll have a real one in my real garage again. Until then, I can rest assured that many people all over the world share my love for Beetles. In fact, my fate has always been determined by this little car, and air cooled Volkswagens as such. I have definitely caught the bug, so to speak.

Thank you, little Beetle!

Thorsten Elbrigmann

Face in the crowd. As familiar as an old friend.

Partner on all adventures. Free like the wind.

Contents:

THE BUG BUG   14–23

Not just one Beetle but an entire hall full. Not just any old hall, but an exact replica of a 1950s Volkswagen repair shop: Richard Hausmann's collection is exceptional.

THE BUTTERFLY   24–31

Who buys a new Beetle convertible, has it beautifully customised and then puts it into storage for 34 years? Thomas Aries, who else! Not the Beetle had to mature, he himself had to.

LIKE FATHER, LIKE SON   32–39

Régis Mathieu's chandeliers hang in the world's great palaces. He also restores Beetles, together with his son Arthur. A real Father and Son Thing.

WELL-MATCHED RIGHT FROM THE START   40–45

A 1948 Beetle that has spent its entire life in Switzerland! With the typical Swiss attention to detail, André Birrer takes good care of this rare car.

MAXIMUM SLOWNESS   46–53

Life at a more relaxed pace in a Beetle with a folding sunroof – that's what racing driver Maximilian Götz looks forward to. His family and friends, and also his small dog Mimi, keep him grounded. On tour through Franconia.

FRIVOLOUS IMPERTINENCE   54–59

Inge Feltrinelli had a dream: to travel the world as a photographer. That is exactly what she did in her Beetles – meeting Ernest Hemingway, Fidel Castro and many others along the way. An epic journey.

DELUXE "SPARKÄFER" VW 1200 – THE FRUGAL MODEL   60–65

Oliver Zinnkann waited for his dream Beetle for many years. Finally, its owner agreed to sell it. The start of an unusual conversion story, with a script by Karl Meier.

THE JOY OF DISCOVERY   66–71

The odd Volkswagen gem has been found in Sweden. However, Göran Thulin's 1951 Beetle is a gem amongst gems with an amazing history and beautiful accessories.

EXPULSION FROM PARADISE   72–77

One owner kept it in his living room, the next buried it beneath old tyres in the yard. Martin Walter's little split rear window Beetle has certainly had a colourful history with a happy end!

THE BARN FIND   78–87

Policeman Florian Ücker employed all his detecting skills to find out what lay behind the village legend of a forgotten Beetle in a barn in the vineyards – which turned out to be true! He rescued it.

MARLENA AND THE LONG DISTANCE RELATIONSHIP   88–95

America is a big and wonderful country. With enough room for two Beetles in the family. Chris Latshaw keeps one in Colorado and one in California: Marlena.

NEW BEGINNINGS IN PEACETIME   96–103

When Germany's first international motor show, the Internationale Automobil-Ausstellung (IAA), after the war was held in Frankfurt am Main in 1951, Volkswagen came up with an amazing trade show stand design.

PLAYROOM HEROES   104–109

Beetle model cars made by Siku, Majorette, Hot Wheels – they were toy box stars once. Now scuffed and dented, well-loved, they bear the scars of thousands of wild races. Christian Blanck photographs them just as they are. Click!

GLOBETROTTERS   110–119

From Vienna around the world in a Beetle – a dream which Dominikus and Zainab Hocher fulfilled themselves. Personal highlight: tying the knot in California.

MANHATTAN TRANSFER   120–131

He earned the money for his Beetle as a teenager by mowing other people's lawns. Donald Morisette and his Volkswagen have been a team ever since. On the streets of New York – and in the classroom.

HEAD OVER HEELS WITH THE ROUND LITTLE CAR   132–139

It's all his dad's fault. He told Kimo Sanchez from Ecuador to brew beer. Kimo now delivers his creations in a small, hugely stubborn red Beetle.

FAITHFUL COMPANIONS TO THE LIMIT   140–147

Winter in Hamburg – for Erik Brandenburg, the conditions couldn't be more perfect for taking his jacked-up Beetles off-road. Mud and snow are his métier.

FROM KIWIS TO BISCUITS   148–153

From London through Europe and the Balkan countries to Turkey, and on through Iran and Pakistan to India. Kiwis Beth and Ivan Hodges did this amazing trip in their Beetle. Twice. With 35 years in between.

HARVEST TIME   154–161

You need to find the Beetle that is perfect for you. However, what makes it perfect? Andrea and Sascha Ahrens' main criterion was not the condition of the car but the year of manufacture. It didn't matter how difficult the restoration would turn out to be.

THE HEART OF A BOXER   162–169

The Ruhr district was shaped by steel and coal. Wolfgang Doetsch and his "electrified" Beetle are proof that the future is already here.

TRIP DOWN MEMORY LANE   170–175

When Sussi and Carsten Andersen open the doors to their museum, it is like stepping back in time. The Danish couple collects Volkswagens – including many Beetles – and shares its passion with the museum visitors.

HE'S PART OF THE FAMILY   176–181

In Indonesia, what was once an advertising claim is beautiful reality. The same Beetle has been in the Waluyo family since 1962. Two photographs have made it the star of many Beetle rallies.

UNEARTHING THE PAST   182–187

Volkswagen Beetles were built as early as in 1941. Ondřej Brom found one of them and has researched its history, with a little help from the international Beetle collectors' scene. Strength lies in numbers!

SILVER SHADOWS   188–193

Some Beetles were never built, although they should have been! Øystein Asphjell, for example, had always dreamt of creating a very special coupe on a Beetle base. So he did.

L'AMOUR TOUJOURS   194–203

Frenchman Alexandre Arash Djavadian has even smuggled cylinder heads through Iranian customs for his folding sunroof Beetle. Today, the doctor uses it as he does his rounds near Paris.

IMPRINT   208

Travelled all over the world – and always on the same side: the team behind this book about the Volkswagen that moves people on all continents. On the road and in their hearts.

B

Baiersdorf / Germany

The Beetles are parked side by side. The matt finish from the early years after the war next to the curved Lufthansa blue and yellow and smart chrome – optimistic harbingers of a shiny future.

The Bug bug

Fifty-seven-year-old Richard Hausmann was literally spoon-fed an interest in VW Beetles. If he was a good boy and finished all of his peas and baby carrots, a picture of the little car would smile at him from his kids dinner plate at every meal. This was to have a profound effect on his later life.

Richard Hausmann went cold turkey for a year. He managed to bear life without a VW Beetle for twelve months. In 2001, the craving simply became too much. He now suffers from the Bug bug worse than ever before. He is totally smitten, especially when he looks in the rear view mirror and sees the split rear window of an early Beetle. Hausmann's mood becomes even more euphoric, though, when he has managed to track down yet another KdF model and it is parked in his garage at last. Only around sixty of the Kraft durch Freude vehicles built between 1941 and 1944, some with a slightly jacked-up Beetle body like a Kubelwagen, survive today; maybe thirty of them are still roadworthy. The successful manager from Erlangen now owns four of these extremely rare models.

Each of these vehicles has its own special history, of course. The other models in Hausmann's collection also bring back some special memories. However, he doesn't hesitate for a second when he is asked what his favourite car is. "The 1948 Export model, that really is rather special. I still prefer to drive that one more than any of the others", he says. A few moments later, he has the documents for this Beetle in his hands. Yes, its history is certainly interesting.

The car was manufactured on 23 September 1948 and delivered to the company Raffay & Co. in Hamburg that same day. It was registered for the first time on 18 October and was taken off the road again exactly three years later, to the day. "The Beetle was then stored well-protected in a wood shed for decades. Huge bushes had to be dug up to recover it and replanted afterwards. Luckily, the former owner had taken the seats out before the car was put away. That is why all of the Beetle's parts are still the original ones. This applies to the engine, gearbox, axles, brakes – and also to the beautifully preserved seats. On top of that, the car hasn't even been welded anywhere." Hausmann bought the 1948 Export, which does have chrome bumpers, although it doesn't have the trims that were available as an extra at the time, in 2005. After some careful restoration work, the Beetle was on the road again at last two years later. At that point, it only had 16,000 kilometres on the clock. By now, the Beetle has clocked up almost 42,000 kilometres without any problems – almost all of those with Richard Hausmann at the wheel.

Even his first car as an eighteen-year-old was a Beetle, a 1966 "Bahama Blue" VW 1300. It was followed by a 1303 manufactured in

Richard Hausmann in front of his favourite Beetle, still unwelded to this day. The 1948 "Export" model was put in storage on 18 October 1951 and has survived in fantastic condition.

At any moment, the door to the garage might open to admit a VW service mechanic in blue overalls carrying a clipboard: the convertible needs lubricating, the grey Standard needs its regular inspection. Of course, Sir!

1973. However, it was probably the blue rectangular rear window 1957 Beetle with a fabric sliding sunroof that was Richard and Anna's wedding car which finally inspired his longing for truly vintage Beetles. The couple travelled many thousands of kilometres in this car before they sold it in late 1999. "Even back then, I found the months without a Beetle quite difficult. However, it was probably fate because ultimately, that is how I acquired my first split rear screen model," Hausmann still recalls. He had bought a classic car magazine at the airport in Berlin. In this magazine, he spotted an advertisement for a "lovingly restored split rear window Beetle, first OTR in 12/51, green, folding sunroof, 25,000 euros." The car stood in the showroom of a VW dealer in Hof. "Even the first impression in March 2001 was super. A few signs of wear and tear, but otherwise all original. Only the carpets and the battery cover were later replacement copies."

The seller supplied the reason for the car's almost perfect condition. The restored Beetle had stood in the showroom for the past thirty years and had only been driven from time to time in the summer. It did not take him long to make up his mind to buy the car. The price also included a beautifully preserved three-piece set of original suitcases for the space behind the fold-down rear bench seat.

Of course, this split rear window Beetle still lives in Hausmann's only recently finished garage today. As the 57-year-old could not find a suitable home for his collection, he had a new building constructed that is based on VW's old specifications for their repair shops. It now houses eleven Beetles, one more interesting than the next, from the 1950 Hebmüller to the two military Beetles from 1946 (French army) and 1948 (British Army of the Rhine).

The small garage has become a **home-from-home for any classic car fan, equipped as it is with all sorts of accessories from the early days of Volkswagen.**

However, these days, Hausmann is particularly interested in the even older so-called KdF Beetles. He spotted his first Type 60 – as VW called the model – for sale in 2009 and bought it immediately. "During the restoration, it turned out to be an exceptionally original example of the few surviving KdFs," the collector says, still delighted by his purchase. "The car was one of nine identically constructed vehicles that were delivered to Berlin on 29 May 1943. Unfortunately, it is now impossible to determine where exactly the vehicle with the design number 519 was used. What is clear is that it ended up with a dealer in Pforzheim in the late 1950s, where it was superficially restored and then exhibited in the showroom for around fifty years."

Hausmann had the car completely overhauled, which revealed some good news as well as some bad: the bonnets and doors turned out to be original but it seemed as if a new engine had been put in, at some point. However, what followed was a sheer incredible stroke of good fortune: "I was in the USA on business, and was offered an old Beetle engine there. It originally came from one of the other eight KdF vehicles that were delivered to Berlin on that same day!" Hausmann immediately bought the engine, took it apart, carried the various parts as his hand luggage and brought his invaluable find to Germany in this way, where it has since powered the amazingly original Beetle without any problems.

In any case, 2009 was a very special year for the now 57-year-old. For a start, he completed an incredibly eventful trip from Erlangen to Peking with some fellow split rear window Beetle enthusiasts. In Moscow, on the way into the Chinese capital where the CEO of Siemens was based at the time, he heard a rumour about another vintage Beetle supposedly owned by a journalist who wanted to sell it.

It took two years, during which Hausmann learned a lot about the Russian mentality and also became something of a Russia-expert for KdF Beetles, before he could finally call the vehicle, which had originally surfaced in St Petersburg, his own. By then, word of Hausmann's interest in the rare Beetle models had already got as far as Lithuania, where a model built during the Second World War had been mounted on a roof and served as an illuminated advertisement for a garage for many years. This car now also lives in the garage near Erlangen. It is safe to assume that more KdF Beetles will follow. For Richard Hausmann, they are not so much witnesses of a dark era in German history but rather collectors' pieces with international fans united by one language: Volkswagen Beetle.

♥

A Hebmüller is parked in front of the just completed hall which was carefully constructed on the basis of original old plans for official VW repair shops.

Model e.g. Type 60
Year of manufacture 1943
Location Baiersdorf
Country Germany
Owned by Richard Hausmann

M

Minden / Germany

The butterfly

Not much more than one kilometre a year – that is all the beautiful convertible owned by Thomas Aries has been driven. Even that is a purely mathematical figure, as the 1303 spent more than 34 years in hibernation before it was resurrected. With only 42 kilometres on the clock, it was biding its time inside a cocoon – not so much in expectation of its own metamorphosis but simply waiting until its owner had completed his.

"You could almost say we saved each other for each other." That is the easiest way to describe the relationship between Thomas Aries and his Beetle, which he bought new in the summer of 1979. On the day of his 27th birthday, he paid for the stunningly beautiful convertible that caught everyone's attention as Thomas had numerous extras fitted when he ordered it.

"I wanted a VW exactly according to my specifications – regardless of what that would cost me," the architect says emphatically. He was determined to own one of the last convertible Beetles before VW moved on to next generation, convertible Golfs. "The second rear view mirror or the sports wheels were basically almost standard extras at the time," says Berliner Thomas Aries, who also treated himself to green tinted windows. "How-

ever, the dealer did a double take when I also wanted a parking heater fitted and ordered a customised paint job. But I was the customer and therefore always right," he adds, winking.

Accordingly, he was allowed to pick a colour usually reserved for Merc owners, and the Beetle was duly painted anthracite metallic grey at the Karmann factory in Osnabrück. "A friend of mine had a Mercedes that colour. I thought it would look amazing together with the green windows."

These were actually rather small details compared to the modifications he commissioned Günter Artz from the legendary dealership "Autohaus Nordstadt" to undertake after he had taken delivery of the car. "I had them fit electric window regulators and had the wheel rims and the additional headlight bowls painted the same colour as the car." The convertible was also equipped with a magnetic lock for the engine cover – underneath which a souped up 86 bhp two litre boxer engine from Oettinger soon found a home. "When I finally stood in front of the finished car, I was so happy I almost cried. It was simply perfect. Exactly as I had imagined it." Nothing to stop him from spending many wonderful hours behind its wheel. However, Thomas Aries made a different, albeit tough, decision. He put the Beetle in storage without driving it even just one metre. For 34 years.

His voice trembles a little when talks about the autumn of 1979, when his perfect 1303 Beetle was waiting for him, at last. All he would have had to do is to get in and turn the ignition key, the car was ready. "Of course I was tempted, no question about it. But I knew myself. And I knew that the way I drove back then did not exactly bode a carefree

Thomas Aries is the first owner of this Volkswagen 1303 convertible with numerous extras, such as a powerful Oettinger engine and a customised paint job – and an unusual story all about extraordinary self-control.

life for the convertible. After all, I was a notorious 'Road Rambo'. When I think back to how I treated our Standard Beetle at the time, I am still ashamed." So Thomas Aries made a decision which some people found ridiculous but many others respected him for. "Whatever you do, don't give me they keys! Put it away – until I can control myself better!" Words that reflect an almost brutally honest self-assessment. The car was therefore put into safe storage on 9 November 1979, carefully jacked up and sent on its silent journey through the decades in a perfectly air-conditioned plastic tube, always hoping that its owner would finally "grow up". Nobody could guess that it would take more than 30 years, not even Thomas himself.

"Alone the feeling of owning a convertible straight out of the factory filled me with pride," he now says about the time his Sleeping Beauty spent dreaming of being driven along twisting country roads. "I hadn't set myself a date for its resurrection," he insists. "I knew that the right moment would simply come." He visited his car from time to time but always felt that the time was not ripe yet. With a sigh, he continued to wait. For 34 years. Like the Beetle did.

The boy racer had matured into a sensible slightly more than middle-aged man when he received a piece of news that would be a

On the road at last! A full 34 years after he purchased it, Thomas finally felt mature enough for the Beetle. A boy racer no longer, he has been on the road in it ever since. Only in good weather, of course!

Enjoying the summer. That is what the 1303 LS with its open character was made for. The Lemmerz sports wheels were an extra at the time, the customised paint job was not, Thomas acknowledges with a smile.

kind of wakeup call for him and his Beetle: "In February 2014, our dance teacher died very suddenly. And that is when you realise that anything could happen, at our age," the enthusiastic dancer Aries reckons. He felt that the right moment had finally come.

All he needed to do to resurrect the car was make one phone call; it took only a few days to wake the Beetle from its deep sleep. The convertible was on the road just in time for the start of the 2014 season, almost exactly 35 years after it had been delivered. "When I finally actually sat in it, I felt like a little boy," Thomas Aries says, recalling the moment with pure delight, even though he knows that due to its low mileage, he could have sold his little gem for a lot of money. "I could easily have bought an identical model with the same extras for the money – and I would still have

had enough left over to keep me in fuel for the rest of my days. But that wouldn't have been MY convertible, the one I had waited for for so long. You can't express that feeling in money."

Thomas Aries laughs when he thinks about it: "Some cars are thrashed for 30 years and then treated with kid gloves. Its the other way round with my one. It was treated with kid gloves for 30 years and will now be thrashed," he reckons, although one shouldn't take this statement to literally. After all, even just stating that he drives the car carefully would be a ridiculous understatement. No trace of "thrashing". Thomas has long since outgrown his boy racer days. For good.

Today, just turning the ignition key already means pure joy for him. He no longer feels the urge to drive hard and fast. "The chugging noise alone is unique," the VW fan, who is certain that he chose the right moment for the car's resurrection, says enthusiastically. "I waited for quite a long time, maybe," he admits, "but not too long, either," he reckons as he gently strokes across a piece of chrome trim, lost in thought. It is still as shiny as it was on the first day. Not exactly miraculous, considering its history. However, that is exactly what it is: a miracle. ♥

Model VW 1303 LS convertible
Year of manufacture 1979
Location Minden
Country Germany
Owned by Thomas Aries

A gem on wheels. This Beetle truly is one! One of the very last convertibles ever built was allowed to hibernate for decades in original condition. Crazy? Not at all; in fact rather fortunate.

G

Gargas / France

Like father, like son

In the glorious landscape of Provence, Régis Mathieu looks after his collection of VW Beetles – called "Coccinelles" in France – with plenty of passion and dedication. His son Arthur is currently restoring his own Type 11. A red-hot passion – that keeps on burning!

Apt in southern France is a typical Provencal village with a pretty church spire, sun-kissed alleyways and impressive views across the mountainous landscape of the Lubéron – well-known for its ochre rock formations and the velvety-soft glow of the sun in the evening. In the spring, countless bees and beetles whizz around the nearby lavender fields. However, a fully grown "Coccinelle", as the VW Beetle has been lovingly named in France, tends to be a rare sight in this corner of the country. If one does turn up, the locals usually know straight away who owns the car that makes such a charming rattling noise: Régis Mathieu!

The businessman and designer is not only well-known in the region for his enthusiasm for cars but above all for his exquisite craftsmanship. Chandeliers and imaginative lighting objects made by Mathieu hang

in the Kremlin, the White House and the Palace of Versailles. The lustrous crystal, brass and gem creations are handmade and artfully displayed at the "Mathieu Lustrerie" – an old ochre factory on the edge of Apt – often together with Régis' exquisite collection of classic cars.

It all started in 1971 with a VW 1302. Régis was only seventeen years old at the time, but the ambitious boy already knew exactly what he wanted: to make his father's small chandelier factory world-famous, and to collect cars. He was particularly smitten by the little round Volkswagens and by Porsche 356s. Régis takes an old black and white photograph off his office wall that shows him as a teenager, kneeling in front of the engine of his first VW Beetle. "Even as a child, I loved Coccinelles. I always wanted to drive my own Beetle one day, and I fulfilled myself this dream as soon as I came of age." The start of a great love affair that lasts to this day. At the Lustrerie, five Beetles share a specially converted factory hall with two VW Karmann Ghias, two T1 vans, a Type 181 courier vehicle, a Formula Vee racing car and several rare Porsches. His favourite is "Mathilde", a dark blue oval rear window 1955 Beetle with only one previous careful lady owner. It still shines like new. It was Régis' present to his wife on her 40th birthday.

The passion for Beetles runs in the family. Régis' 14-year-old son Arthur is already following in papa's footsteps. He bought himself his first own Beetle four months ago. A light grey Type 11 from Portugal. A 1959 model in unrestored original condition, rust-free, with the original finish, hardly driven. A rare find. Arthur snapped it up. His sister Inès and her boyfriend Charles are helping him to restore it. Papa has passed the "Bug bug" on to them, he admits with a smile. Arthur

Arthur Mathieu is just fourteen years old – yet he already owns a 1959 Beetle he imported from Portugal with the help of his father Régis, his sister Inès and her boyfriend Charles.

The technology has had a complete overhaul, but the vintage charm has been preserved.

Beetle in his heart, his eye on a Porsche: **Arthur is smitten by the old Beetle-based Formula V racer. His father's chandeliers hang in the Kreml, the White House and the Palace of Versailles.**

wants to start his own Beetle collection, together with Charles. The boys have big plans.

The engine has already been reconditioned and is now gleaming, the carburettor still has to be replaced, the paintwork has to be touched up here and there and the reddish brown leather seats need a few patches. However, Arthur doesn't want to do too much. It is important to him to retain the patina and to leave the Beetle in a condition that is as original as possible. "Because they're worth more money like that", Arthur knows. Arthur is also particularly proud of the Beetle's original accessories, the manual and a small tool roll he found in the boot of the car. It was covered in grime, but after a few hours of cleaning it with a toothbrush, the boy managed to reveal the same pale blue imitation leather that was used for the car's interior. Arthur carefully pulls the dinky spanners out from underneath the loops that hold them in place. They look as if they belong to a toy car.

Admittedly, as he is only fourteen years old, Arthur is not yet allowed to drive his Beetle. However, there is a short dirt track in the grounds of the Mathieu Lustrerie where Arthur can at least drive the car for a few hundred metres. He is therefore really looking forward to his first proper outings with his friend Charles, who is already nineteen. "We will definitely go on a few super tours in the Beetle. I can hardly wait." In a few months' time, Arthur will also be allowed to drive the car on public roads as a learner – provided he is accompanied by his father. Not that he actually needs to practice much, Arthur already has plenty of practical driving experience. Sitting on his father's lap, Arthur already steered a Porsche Carrera GTS at a classic car rally when he was only five years old. They won.

The talented boy has been practicing for this summer's first race in Le Mans in his father's Formula Vee. An exception to the rule, as Régis emphasises, because for as long as Arthur is still at school, homework takes precedence over his racing passion. Arthur wants to be an architect one day, although another goal is much more important to him, of course. As soon as the first Beetle is finished, he intends to start on the next one. By the time he turns eighteen, in three years' time, Arthur plans to have restored enough Beetles to make his big dream come true: a Porsche 356 Speedster of his own. Just like his father. ♥

Model Type 11
Year of manufacture 1959
Location Gargas
Country France
Owned by Arthur Mathieu

History does repeat itself. **Régis often recognises himself in his son. Looking at the old photo from his wild youth, you immediately realise why.**

L

Lucerne / Switzerland

Well-matched right from the start

The sunlight gently caresses the Pearl Grey paintwork and gives it a silky matt lustre. The valve radio makes a buzzing noise, the boxer quietly whispers something about 25 bhp. What André Birrer appreciates most when he drives his 1948 Beetle is the muted soundtrack.

The clock of the small church strikes six times. The evening sun makes everything cast long shadows on this early summer's day. June, fragrant flowers, the Swiss mountains – an idyll. In the middle of all this, the domed roof of a Beetle. With its inconspicuous Pearl Grey finish, it looks as if it doesn't want to disturb the well-balanced arrangement of wooden houses, meadows and meandering paths. It actually contributes to this harmony. Just like it always has done, as it has spent its entire life here. It was built in Wolfsburg on 8 October 1948 and delivered to the Swiss importer AMAG in Zurich only ten days later.

André Birrer knows every bolt on his Beetle. He restored it a few years ago and now looks after the car and appreciates it. The very early Beetles have an extremely purist dashboard. Two storage compartments on the right and left outer corners. In between, two recess-

es: on the left, space for the speedometer unit including all switches and the ignition and on the right, a space that is either covered by a plain sheet metal plate with the gear diagram or can hold a clock or – if the money stretched to this – a radio. André Birrer smiles and gently caresses his Beetle's radio, a Blaupunkt Volkswagen valve radio Type A610B. He turns the left Bakelite button until he hears a soft click. The scale starts to glow and soon lights up. A quiet electric humming announces that the radio valves on the inside of the box are heating up; finally, a buzzing noise comes out of the round speaker covered in ivory white mesh that stays almost constant, regardless of which frequency André selects with the radio's right-hand button. "Most of the stations no longer transmit," he says sadly. Most medium wave transmitters were switched off in 2015. France Info, France Bleu and Deutschlandradio were some of the last major European radio stations to go off the air. There are only a few stations that still transmit on medium wave, although the reception is very poor. In future, medium wave will serve as a backup maritime navigation system should GPS fail. André would have to travel as far as to the USA with his Beetle; medium wave is still of some importance there.

A radio as a relic in a Volkswagen that is around 70 years old and still works as perfectly as the Beetle itself. The car still has its original engine, gearbox and axles, and plenty of the original bodywork has also survived, despite the fact that it has not always been driven too carefully, even though it has never left Switzerland. The Beetle spent the last years of its first life, pre-restoration, in a gravel quarry where it was used as a transport vehicle. Then André rescued the poor car, dam-

André Birrer restored his 1948 Beetle himself. The little car has even been mistreated in a gravel quarry, and still survived the ordeal intact. It waves a friendly goodbye with its aerial.

PHOTOS STEFAN BAU   TEXT THORSTEN ELBRIGMANN

The dashboard and seats are of a simplicity that is movingly beautiful. Switches for the lights, the wipers and the indicators.
A starter button, a petrol tap in the footwell. Two front seats, a bench seat in the rear. That's it.

aged but not yet completely broken. He was immediately fascinated by the vehicle, which was built at a time when Volkswagen hadn't even begun to distinguish between "Standard" and "Export" models. This distinction was not introduced until 1949. There was only the "Volkswagen". Period. However, vehicles destined to be exported to the Netherlands or Switzerland, for example, were somewhat prettified. Chrome bumpers and chrome hubcaps added a little bit of sophistication to the split rear window Beetle made in Wolfsburg.

The technology was still at the pre-war level: mechanical cable brakes, non synchromesh gearbox, a petrol tap and a wooden measuring stick in the boot for determining the amount of fuel left in the tank. A first tentative attempt at a card bonnet liner was all that was introduced to improve the driving comfort. André Birrer shrugs and simply drives it as it is. For him, his Beetle is a comfort zone just the way it left the factory. Despite all its simplicity. The headlights and the small round tail lights are powered by a 6 volt battery. Semaphore indicators located between the doors and the rear windows sig-

nal a change of direction; one centrally fitted orange-coloured brake light indicates that the driver is attempting to stop the car. The speedometer promises 120 km/h, but the little car never actually reaches such speeds. Its maximum speed is just over 100 km/h – and that is enough. Then the gearbox starts to scream, the boxer puts its nose to the grindstone, and you can see the pleasure in the eyes of the passers-by, other drivers and also in the eyes of André, who loves this Beetle. At least as much as his fellow boxer 1955 VW Transporter pick-up, which is often parked next to the Beetle.

The charm of such old Volkswagens probably lies in their authentic simplicity. André agrees, although this simplicity can also be quite tricky. It is anything but easy to find spare parts for vehicles as old as these. That is also why the restoration took such a long time, because there were always parts missing. However, the international collectors' scene communicates and collectors help each other out. Regardless of what is missing, an exhaust, a headlight chrome trim, a window seal or the card bonnet lining: the missing part will have survived, somewhere in the world. Somewhere. You just have to find it.

The sun is sinking lower towards the horizon, almost touching the mountains. Time to drive back to the garage. He pushes the starter button in the middle of the dashboard, and the engine starts almost straight away. The headlights come on. André reverses, though, rolls down onto the road, and takes another turn around the village. The church clock strikes, the boxer's growl becomes quieter. The smell of fir trees, the humming of bees. Everything in perfect harmony, like yin and yang. Like André Birrer and his Beetle. ♥

Model VW Type 11
Year of manufacture 1948
Location Canton of Lucerne
Country Switzerland
Owned by André Birrer

As thick as thieves: Besides the Beetle, André Birrer also owns a very early VW Transporter. It has been restored just as meticulously and is always happy to socialise with its fellow VW.

U

Uffenheim / Germany

MAXimum slowness

Dark hair, a cheerful laugh, a heavy local dialect: meet Maximilian Götz. Passionate racing driver. Ambitious to the point of no return. Ridiculously fast. Ridiculously successful. He relaxes from the hustle and bustle of the racing circuit with his family, and with his 1961 folding sunroof Beetle.

Starting grid, Nürburgring: he puts his helmet on several times, pulls on his racing gloves, first the left one, then the right one. Adjusts his glasses below the visor. Sharpens his senses, begins to concentrate. As soon as he is strapped into the six point harness that ties him to the bucket seat, he focuses on one thing only, the perfect racing line – and on winning. Full blast, that's just what he's like, anything else would seem pointless to Maximilian Götz. All or nothing. Now or never! Or, to put it in his words and the motto of his fan community: #MAXimumAttack.

Max was born in Lower Franconia and is a racing driver; he raced in the DTM for the past two years before recently returning to the ADAC GT Masters race series. He is well-known there; this is where he feels at home. He already won the ADAC GT Masters championship in 2012; he also won the Total 24 Hours of Spa in 2013, for example. In 2014, he won the Blancpain Sprint Series in a SLS AMG GT3. The 32-year-old with the yellow Mamba now competes in the MANN-FILTER Team HTP Motorsport as well as in the Blancpain GT Series with the Mercedes-AMG Team STRAKKA. Racing bolides with sheer unlimited power.

Starting grid, Uffenheim: his Beetle has 34 bhp. That is 523 fewer than his everyday car made in Affalterbach, a Mercedes-AMG GT C Roadster Edition 50. "A Beetle has always been one of my dream cars. The embodiment of relaxed life in the slow lane," Max sums up his decision to buy the Beetle eight years ago. The Beetle represents what is called "quality time" these days. It allows him to reconnect with himself, with the family. He parks the car outside his brother Basti's front door and moves over. To the passenger seat. A rare occurrence, but he says he enjoys it when his little brother is at the wheel. "Basti has an unusually good feel for cars; I like sitting next to him when he is driving," says Max. They trust each other, you can feel that as soon as you get into the back seat. That is exactly what their parents Heike and Addy have always instilled in their three boys: the family must stick together, that is the most important thing. It is therefore hardly surprising that Grandma Götz is waiting for them at home with freshly baked muffins after hearing that they were planning an outing in the Beetle. Max and Basti are cruising through the Lower Franconia wine region and talk about their dreams for the future. Staying healthy, of course, and the hall where they park their cars has to become even more characterful, become an established meeting place for friends and family. "Home and family are very important to us, that's what

Maximilian Götz usually drives racing cars with 500-plus bhp. However, when he is at home and has the time, he relaxes in his Beetle, enjoying the sunshine – whilst Jack Russell terrier Mimi hunts for mice in the hay.

On the way to his brother Basti s house; he is going to be Max s chauffeur for the day.

The family dog is waiting! **Mimi likes the Beetle. She can stick her head out of the folding roof, loves the green-tinted shade supplied by the external sun visor – all that is needed now is a personalised number plate, "W-OOF".**

we learnt from our parents," they both agree. Jack Russell terrier bitch Mimi, the family dog, is also in the car, of course.

"The Beetle embodies German engineering, the general sense of optimism that prevailed at the time. It is an icon. Unfortunately, you see far too few of them on the roads; I often wonder where all the Beetles have got to. What I love about it? It doesn't matter how long the car has stood in the garage, as soon as I turn the key, it starts," he continues and laughs because if it didn't start straight away, Basti would immediately be there to sort it out. Basti is a master vehicle technician and works at the Porsche centre in Würzburg as a service consultant. "He is a perfectionist and drives extremely carefully; he is almost overprotective," Max says about his 29-year-old brother, who in turn calls him a lout and a nut, albeit not seriously. Sure. Basti often comes along to his big brother's races, and their father Addy, who used to race himself and took Max along to the Norisring in Nuremberg when he was only seven years old, always joins him. Max's first trip to a go kart track, on the other hand, was his mother Heike's idea: "My father was totally against it, so I kept on nagging my mother until she made this dream of mine come

true when Addy was out." That was in 1996. Max was hooked. He was going to be a racing driver when he grew up. His idols: Bernd Schneider and Michael Schumacher.

In his childhood and youth, the talented go kart driver had the opportunity to compete against stars like Nico Rosberg; in 2003, he won the Formula BMW ahead of Sebastian Vettel; two years later, Max drove in Lewis Hamilton's team in the Formula Three. As a precision driver in the Formula 1 movie *Rush*, he was Daniel Brühl's double in a few of the scenes where Niki Lauda thunders across the screen wheel against wheel with other cars. He soon made a name for himself, is considered to be a particularly good team player and reliable, ambitious and confident. He is the kind of guy who doesn't give up. Not any longer.

Max did give it up once in all those years and quit professional racing: "I thought I just couldn't carry on," he says. He is not talking about his skills but is referring to the financial means that are so important in motorsport. In 2009, he opened a little bar called the "Schlawiner-Bar" in his home town Uffenheim together with his brothers Basti and Moritz. He worked behind the bar, with a clear mind, filling glasses. A nice hobby for someone who has been passionate about motorsport since childhood, but hardly fulfilling. He clawed his way back, as an instructor and as a racing driver, found sponsors and supporters. "For many years, I didn't always have the best material available to me, but that's different now, luckily."

Luckily for him, he also has another life away from the race track. His smartphone rings; he apologises, they have to go, his fellow firefighters are waiting, he forgot about the time. Quickly, they park the Beetle next to the Samba van, get into the Mercedes-AMG GT C Roadster and leave for a meeting of the local voluntary fire brigade about the duty roster. ♥

Model Type 11
Year of manufacture 1961
Location Uffenheim
Country Germany
Owned by Maximilian Götz

The Franconian vineyards invite you to just keep on driving into the sunset; the cooling fan stirs up dust – a perfect summer's day outing in the sun yellow Beetle.

M

Milan / Italy

Frivolous impertinence

Inge Schönthal's fortunes have often been determined by luck, courage and meeting the right partner at the right time. In the 1950s, she explored the world as a photojournalist – in her Beetle, which also finally carried her from Hamburg to Milan, and towards a completely different life.

Inge Schönthal didn't fit the mould. She was born in Essen in late 1930. Inge grew up in Göttingen at a time that was the most unfortunate in history for the daughter of a Jew and a German. Her parents separated when she was eight years old, and her father fled from the Nazis to the Netherlands. Her mother soon married a German officer, and Inge simply couldn't wait to grow up, despite the fact that in the years after the war, women were mainly expected to have children, take care of their husband and keep house.

Inge was different. She wanted to explore the world, meet people and hear their stories. She decided to become a photojournalist, which would allow her to satisfy her curiosity, travel and earn money, all at the same time. The ideal job, and also an extremely unusual one for a young woman back then. At the age of nineteen, she packed her things, got on her bike and cycled all the way to Hamburg in search of Rosemarie Pierer, a pioneer of multi-image photography. Multi-image photography consisted of several slides being projected onto different fields to create one work of art; it was considered extremely avant-garde. Today, it would probably be called multi-media performance art. That is exactly what Inge wanted to do, so she began to train as a photographer. At the beginning, she lived in the vestibule of the studio's darkroom and owned only the mattress she slept on. However, the pretty girl knew how to get on in life and earned extra money with modelling jobs.

By chance, she was approached by Hans Huffzky, editor-in-chief of the women's magazine *Constanze*, in 1951. As she wore a camera around her neck, he simply assumed that she was a photographer. Huffzky happened to be in desperate need of photojournalists, preferably female ones as the editorial office was staffed mainly by men. He offered Inge a job straight away, even though he found her photographs of ships in the port of Hamburg, for example, rather dreadful. From now on, she would photograph people. What a stroke of luck for Inge, to be contracted by what was then Germany's best-known and biggest women's magazine.

A year later, she made another dream come true: she bought herself her own motor car. However, she didn't want any old car but the car that got Germany driving. In 1952, around 100,000 Beetles, then simply called Volkswagens, had already come off the production line in Wolfsburg. Inge's new passport to freedom was one of them, blue and "topless", to match her "frivolous impertinence", as she herself liked to describe her approach. It was also better than a fixed roof (which

Inge Feltrinelli was not born to "la dolce vita". She had a long way to go before she could afford her first Beetle, which then carried her to wherever she was able to practice the art of photography. A loyal companion.

PHOTOS INGE FELTRINELLI/ FOTOGLORIA   TEXT TINA GALLACH

she treated herself to later on). The beautiful young lady did not mince her words, which was unusual at the time but certainly gained her respect, especially in her male-dominated profession.

She was now mobile. She was able to travel to her photo shoots, go on holiday and go to the parties attended by the stars of her era, Germany's "economic miracle" years. The country was in the grip of a general sense of optimism, and Inge Schönthal knew she was pursuing the path that was right for her. Hans Huffzky had also introduced her to important people in the world of publishing, and she soon knew a lot of celebrities, including the actor Gérard Philipe, who happened to be touring Germany at the time. Inge thought that he resembled the irrepressible folklore prankster Till Eulenspiegel, so she drove him to a town around 50 kilometres to the east of Hamburg to show him the Till Eulenspiegel sculpture there – in her convertible Beetle, of course. Gérard Philipe was enchanted, by the progressive lady and by her vehicle, whose outstanding finish particularly impressed the Frenchman.

Her career took off, and in 1954, she was permitted to visit Cuba. *Constanze* had commissioned her to do a piece about Ernest Hemingway. The era's greatest author lived at the "Finca Vigía", around 20 kilometres away from Havana. However, after an adventurous journey via New York City and Miami, in part by car (although probably not by Beetle), Hemingway turned out to be unavailable. She waited for him in Havana, with 120 Deutschmarks in her pocket, until he had time for her – and what times they had when he finally showed up. A selfie taken with her Rolleiflex with the aid of a tripod and a flash went around the world and made Schönthal famous. The photo shows the 55-year-old pas-

sionate deep-sea fisherman Hemingway in a T-shirt and vest, Inge in a revealing dress and between them, a 30 kilo swordfish – taken out of an ice box extra for the staged photo. Originally, there were three people in the photograph. However, the magazines simply cut Hemingway's boatswain Gregorio, the inspiration for his bestseller *The Old Man and the Sea*, out of the picture. Another world-famous photo of Hemingway was also taken during her fortnight's stay at the Hemingway finca. The photo shows the great man sleeping on the floor of his living room.

The fish photo, although not perfectly lit, opened all doors for Schönthal, and she was permitted to photograph media-shy Picasso, as well as Marc Chagall, Édith Piaf and other stars of the decade. One of Inge Schönthal's maxims was that an image doesn't have to be pin-sharp. She believed that it was all about the decisive moment when the shutter is released. A decisive moment of a different kind occurred on 14 July 1958. On that

day, she met the Italian publisher, intellectual and billionaire Giangiacomo Feltrinelli at a party in Hamburg. After the party, she drove him to his hotel. It wasn't love at first sight – not like with her Beetle. However, things developed rapidly and in late 1958, the time had come for what would probably be Schönthal's last big trip in her Beetle. Inge drove the 1,250 kilometres from Hamburg to Milan to start her new life reassured by the friendly growl of the air cooled four-cylinder rear-mounted boxer, along motorways, across mountain passes and past lakes, directly to the Italian fashion and media capital. The marriage took place in Mexico in 1960 and lasted nine years.

Today, the grande dame of the publishing world has been at the helm of the great publishing house Feltrinelli, whose biggest coup was the publication of *Doctor Shivago*, for almost half a century. She is still "Il Presidente" – as she started to call herself shortly after the death of her husband. In the 1970s, she successfully modernised Feltrinelli. Giangi, as he was known to his friends, died in 1972 at the age of 45 in a dynamite explosion. He was a well-known communist and close to Fidel Castro. It has never been established whether his death was an accident or whether he was murdered. Their son Carlo, born in 1962, is now the company's "big boss", as Inge calls him. However, she still lends a hand with the company, at trade fairs and sometimes also behind the wheel of the car in which she discovered the world, usually frivolously and often impertinently. ♥

Her easy-going approach became her trademark. Inge Feltrinelli's pictures showed some of the world's greatest personalities – such as Fidel Castro, for example – in relaxed poses, up close and intimate. By the way, her first Volkswagen was soon followed by a convertible.

Model VW convertible
Year of manufacture 1952
Location Hamburg / Milan
Country Germany / Italy
Owned by Inge Feltrinelli

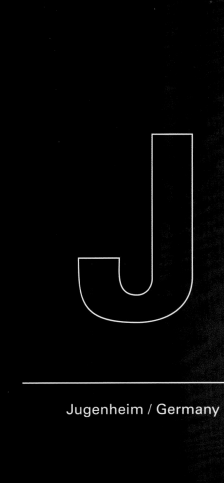

J
_____

Jugenheim / Germany

Deluxe "Sparkäfer" VW 1200 – the frugal model

Sports steering wheel, storage net, go-faster stripes: Kamei sure knew how to upgrade a Beetle. Oli Zinnkann's VW 1200, a classic model marketed as the "Sparkäfer", the frugal edition, is equipped with so many extras that it illustrates Kamei's product range better than any brochure.

Oli Zinnkann had already flirted with a VW 1200 in the mid-90s – even though the knobbly car originally designed in Wolfsburg still came off the production lines in Mexico at the time. On the streets of West Germany, Beetles were a common sight even then; Beetles in good condition were often still in the hands of their first owners. However, it was clear that the heyday of the little car with the rear-mounted engine was gradually coming to a close; far-sighted collectors had long since started to buy up Beetles in good condition. Like this "one careful retired owner" model that was always parked in the same place.

However, the problem was: Oli often saw the Beetle, but never its owner. "I couldn't seem to get hold of him, so I stuck my mobile phone number behind the wipers. I still do that today," the Beetle fan says. At that point

in time, he had long since caught the "Bug bug" and was already tinkering around with a split rear window Beetle.

Nevertheless, he still would have liked to park the orange dream on four wheels in his garage. Unfortunately, the owner didn't contact him. Not a day later, not a month later and not even a year later. His phone did not suddenly ring until thirteen years later, which only goes to show that some things are worth waiting for.

"I had already given up when the owner called me out of the blue in 2010 to sell me the Beetle because he reckoned he was now too old to drive," Oli explains the owner's change of mind after so many years of silence. He still can't quite believe it today, although the previous owner certainly knew what a treasure he had looked after so well for so many years. The mileage alone, a rather modest 77,000 kilometres, said it all.

After some tough negotiations, they finally struck a deal. However, the seller's contract, dated 23 December 2011, did contain some rather strange provisos. Oli was planning to upgrade the Beetle with a few period extras – the collecting of which was another passion of his. He had made no secret of this when he offered to buy the car, which prompted the previous owner to ensure that he could have his say in the matter. He was probably worried that the conversion of his beloved Volkswagen would be too radical.

"I had to meet up with him once a month so he could check the condition of the Beetle. And if I planned any changes, he wanted to be involved in the decisions." Oli reckoned he would be able to live with these provisos; he strictly complied with both, which led to many

Oli Zinnkann is the reincarnation of "accessory god" Karl Meier, who once built everything for the Beetle that had been overlooked or never even thought of in Wolfsburg under the brand name of Kamei.

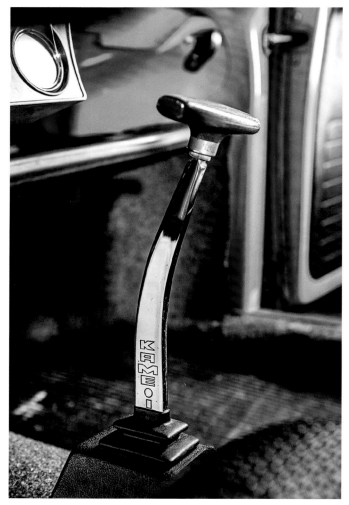

Shift gear faster, sit more beautifully, store away odds and ends – Kamei had everything for Beetles you might possibly want. Even a front spoiler and a gravel guard in a chequered flag design.

enjoyable meetings until the old gentleman passed away. At least he knew that he had left his Beetle in good hands and had seen it gradually evolve into a museum of vintage accessories on four wheels.

The range of modifications started with a classic "quick shift" gear stick with the well-known Kamei logo on the knob. The sports gear stick truly upgrades the interior. The Beetle was gradually equipped with other extras such as headrests, a door lock cover that is supposed to prevent the lock from freezing in the winter, defrost reflector plates, a storage net and a sports steering wheel whilst Oli kept on looking for suitable accessories.

Where Kamei is concerned, the fan from the Rheinhessen region has long since become well-known as an absolute expert; his blog about Kamei parts and other accessories is the first port of call for anyone who's interested in the subject from all over the world. "The demand amongst collectors often leads to me sending parts from my collection which I happen to have twice to some very far away places." These collectors often live in Asia, Australia or North America. Even in Africa, fans are after defrost reflector plates still in their original packaging or other early Kamei products that have been waiting to be fitted for 50 years.

The black Kamei go-faster stripes are particularly rare. In eight years of collecting, Oli has managed to source only three sets; one decorates his own Beetle, even though the previous owner thought them a bit too daring. Ultimately, though, he agreed; he didn't want to "be thought of as intolerant of the youth of today," Oli Zinnkann recalls their drawn-out negotiations regarding this issue. The frugal look of a "Sparkäfer" Beetle, coupled with the sporty opulence of the products made by Karl Meier (Kamei) – a contradictory combination? Certainly. However, one that couldn't be more charming. ♥

Model VW 1200 A "Sparkäfer"
Year of manufacture 1972
Location Jugenheim
Country Germany
Owned by Oli Zinnkann

B

Borås / Sweden

The joy of discovery

Göran Thulin is a Volkswagen fan from Sweden. He is the sort of person who believes that persistence will pay off in the end, which is ultimately why he managed to unearth this 1951 folding roof Beetle. It had stood buried beneath a layer of dust for 25 years – but it was exactly this dust, the fact that it had been forgotten about, that promised joy. It was a stroke of good fortune, for the Beetle and for Göran.

The old barn door opens with a gentle creak. Even just getting the key to turn in the lock had been quite difficult. The grey boards had not been moved in a long time, nor had a human being crossed the threshold of the barn. A gentle ray of sunshine brings a little light into the dusty interior. In the opposite corner, the curved shape of a car can just be made out in its soft glow. No need to see the badge to know what kind of car this is. It's a VW Beetle. Over the years, the apparently black paint had been covered in a thick layer of dust. What remains visible looks dull; no trace of the car's formerly shiny finish. It must have stood here for a very long time; in fact, as it turns out later on: for 25 years. A barn find; the kind of thing you actually only read about in books. Maybe often, but always a different story; always new, always a

new moment of pure joy! You must understand, for a car enthusiast, such moments of joy are incredibly romantic; for a Beetle fan, they are simply the height of emotion.

The story of this find happened in Sweden and, to tell you the truth: it already took place as long ago as 1991. However, even back then, a barn find was considered a rather rare occurrence. This one is as wonderful today as it was back then.

Göran Thulin heard of this buried treasure purely by coincidence. He had owned quite a few Volkswagen cars throughout his life, including the odd classic. Göran was therefore something of an expert, and that is why he knew straight away what he had found: an early 1950s split rear window Beetle. He realised what he was looking at as soon as he discovered the small air vent behind the front wing. Only Beetles manufactured between January 1951 and September 1952 featured an air vent like this one, which was soon rather unflatteringly called a "crotch cooler" in popular parlance. The designers in Wolfsburg had come up with it to improve ventilation inside the Beetle. Their first attempt had been curved apertures in the side windows with small air vents that opened as soon as the window was rolled down a short way, with the windows themselves staying firmly enclosed by their frames. Beetle owners did not respond too enthusiastically to this solution approach, so the VW developers tried it with vents in the front side panels. They could be opened from the inside and released a veritable blast of fresh air into the interior of the Volkswagen. Some people felt that this permanent swish of cold air in the crotch area was anything but pleasant. However, we do not know whether it actually had any ad-

Göran Thulin loves life and his darling Inger. Together, they often go for a drive in their 1951 "crotch cooler" Beetle with folding sunroof, Albert mirrors and a third brake light.

PHOTOS STEPHAN REPKE   TEXT KLAUS MORHAMMER

The large reflectors are a legal requirement in Sweden; the gravel guards are a sensible idea, as anyone knows who has ever driven on northern Sweden's gravel roads.

verse effects on someone's private parts. For the design department, the issue was therefore not quite resolved yet. The final solution was ultimately found in the form of quarter light windows in the doors which the Beetle featured until its last days in July 2003.

Göran's discovery didn't even need the side air vents because as soon as he had blown some of the dust off the Beetle roof, a large sliding sunroof appeared. A split rear window Beetle with a sliding folding sunroof! Göran was completely bowled over. However, he returned home empty-handed. Although he had been able to convince the owner to show him the car, the owner didn't want to sell it to him. For an entire year, Göran persistently tried to convince the old man to part with his treasure – and was finally rewarded for his persistence. The Beetle's previous history revealed some interesting facts. Even though Sweden had already been a strong export market for Volkswagen at quite an early stage, Beetles were no longer a common

sight on Swedish roads in the 1990s, either, and certainly not a 1951 split rear window Beetle. The previous owner had purchased the car in 1965 and then put it away in the aforementioned barn three years later. Sweden introduced regular vehicle roadworthiness inspections in 1968. Göran says that at the time, quite a few Swedes took their cars off the road voluntarily as they were worried that the inspector might confiscate their vehicle. How bizarre, its owner had taken the Beetle off the road because he was worried that it might be taken off the road. Barn. Dust. Sleep. Final destination.

When Göran had a closer look at the Volkswagen, he was hardly able to contain his surprise. The car wasn't missing a single part; it didn't even have any rust perforations. Why had its previous owner been so worried about the inspection? It was no longer possible to find out the answer to this question. However, it was definitely excellent news for its new owner back in 1991. The overhaul, including a new paint job, didn't take long at all and Göran now had the perfect grateful subject for indulging in his second great passion: collecting vintage Volkswagen accessories. The Petri Banjo steering wheel Göran now uses to point his split rear window Beetle in the right direction was an extremely popular choice. He does so to the sounds of a luxurious Becker-Monza radio, one of the particularly expensive extras at the time, especially the high-end version with an integrated clock. Smokers appreciated the ashtray next to the gear stick. It was made by Schenk. For the lady passenger, SHO sold a sun visor in the same style as the visor on the driver side, long before it became available as an optional extra from VW. A fuel gauge was not a standard feature until much later. Before that, it was merely equipped with a reserve fuel tap. A rather rewarding business for accessory suppliers, then. Dehne's fuel gauge was the perfect solution here. Under the rear bonnet, a lovely round Hazet toolbox that is worth a lot of money these days, especially the rare 16-inch version, is clipped to the inside of the spare tyre. The front bonnet hides an equally rare gem: a MAG supercharger made by the former Swiss motorbike manufacturer Motosacoche that adds a few more horse power to the modest Beetle engine. Göran, of course, is not particularly interested in the success of this tuning measure; what matters to him is the enjoyment he gets out of seeing this quite rare and unusual Beetle accessory in situ. The beautiful trim rings around the hubcaps also contribute to this, just like the running board mats, the Hagus rear view mirror, the shiny tailpipe embellisher and a few other bits and pieces. Perfect Beetle Love could look like this, but for Göran, it would never be quite perfect without his beloved companion. His enjoyment of owning a car like this is perfected by driving this dream on four wheels through the Swedish countryside with the folding roof wide open and his Inger by his side. ♥

Intimacy, as offered only by a Beetle, is the most important thing. Over the years, Göran has also collected many accessories to improve the driving comfort, for example a Petri steering wheel and the Dehne fuel gauge fitted between the speedo and the radio.

Model Export Beetle
Year of manufacture 1951
Location Borås
Country Sweden
Owned by Göran Thulin

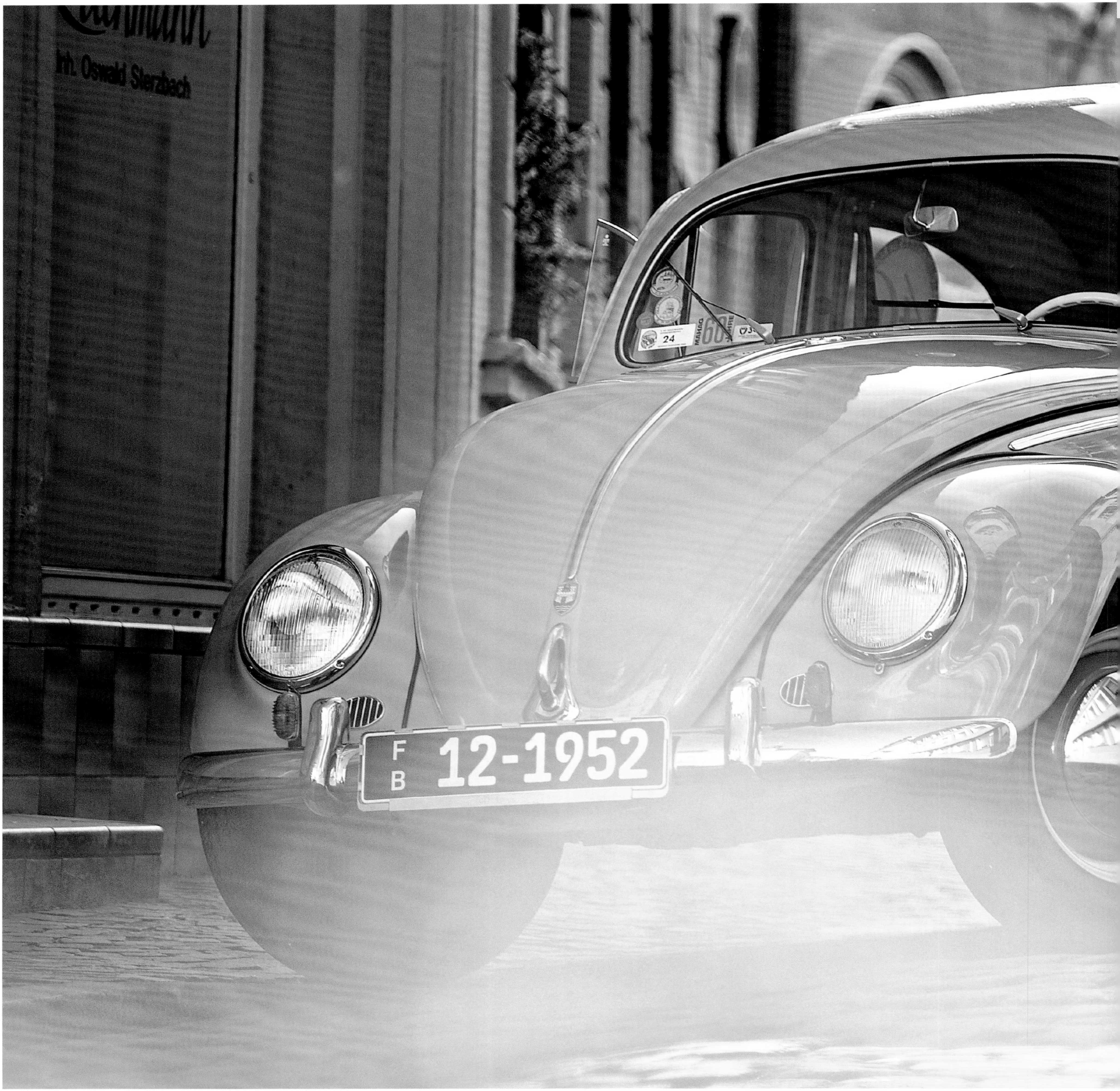
Inh. Oswald Sterzbach
F B 12-1952

R

Rastatt / Germany

Expulsion from Paradise

Buried underneath a mountain of old tyres – that's how Martin Walter saw his Beetle for the first time. However, he was able to rescue this 1952 treasure. A treasure with currently 31,005 kilometres on the clock.

Martin Walter's everyday car needed new tyres, which led him to a backyard garage that sold unused ones at affordable prices: "That's where I spotted a Beetle buried beneath an unbelievably huge mountain of old tyres," he recalls the first moment of a love which, however, would not be consummated for a very long time.

"Of course, you could see that it was an older model. I took a quite few tyres off the Beetle – and soon realised what was parked there, a split rear window model that was largely in original condition. Stored outdoors, with the windows open!" Martin still shudders when he thinks back to this first meeting – which was immediately followed by disappointment. Martin had been looking for a split rear window Beetle for a long time and told the tyre dealer that he would like to buy it. However, the dealer's response was less than encouraging: "With a smug smile, the tyre chap named a ridiculous price! And this from a chap who stores a car like that outdoors. OUTDOORS!"

Which is also where the Beetle remained for the next five years until he went to a classic car meeting in the Alsace in the late summer of 1999. "I struck up a conversation with someone and soon learnt more about 'my' split rear window Beetle, which had been repainted on the outside for selling purposes in the late 80s and then been pushed outside shortly afterwards, in April 1990." Martin now also gained an insight into the actual ownership situation – and after another six months, he was finally able to rescue the historic Beetle.

The car had stood outdoors for almost exactly ten years, from April 1990 to March 2000. Martin's grin nevertheless became increasingly wider during his first inspection of the Beetle, not least because the 27,000 kilometres on the clock turned out to be genuine. "Its actual substance was therefore fantastic. Everything was original, including the exhaust, and in good condition. Pretty unbelievable when you consider the many years it stood outdoors."

After a brief "service", the engine started straight away, as if it had never stood still for so many years. "The original spare tyre was still in its place, and the old grooved semaphore indicators had never been replaced!" Even the upholstery still felt like new: no sagging at all! The single pipe exhaust, clutch, the beaded wings or the heart shaped rear lights had also never been touched in all those years. A sensation!

Martin Walter is a really, really big Beetle fan who can spot a gem like this one even when it is buried underneath a pile of old tyres: a Beetle once delivered to Belgium that was first loved, then buried and finally exhumed.

This Beetle is so rare **because it is a design hybrid, a split rear window model that already featured the oval rear window model dashboard; this version was built for only a few months in 1952.**

As time went by, Martin was able to reconstruct the history of his split rear window Beetle: "The first owner ordered the Beetle in March 1952 from the Belgian importer D'Ieteren Frères in Brussels, an official Volkswagen dealer since 1948," Martin takes up the story. The first buyer had to wait almost nine months for his new Beetle, which came off the Wolfsburg production line on 8 December 1952. It arrived in Brussels two days later and was registered for the first time in Braine-l'Alleud, in the Walloon Brabant region, on 19 December 1952.

Surprisingly, the car was already taken off the road again in 1955. "In the late 1960s, its first owner moved to Mittelbaden – where he kept it in his living room, would you believe it? Apparently, the dear man retired in 1987, and the next year, the VW was sold on with only 25,500 kilometres on the clock." That same year, the Beetle also travelled to the 13th classic car meeting in Baden-Baden – only to be stored outdoors soon afterwards. The Volkswagen was finally swallowed up by a pile of old tyres and disappeared from sight. If there was something like the Expulsion from Paradise for cars, this would have been it.

Looking closely, you can spot that time has left its marks. "However, an almost 70-year-old car like this one is allowed to show its age," emphasises Martin. "And that is also why I would never take it apart for a complete overhaul. A basically unrestored yet still roadworthy split rear window Beetle is a four-wheeled witness to history and as such simply too invaluable to do that!"

Accordingly, he treats the car with due consideration: "I do maybe 200 kilometres a year in this vintage Beetle – extremely carefully, this little gem deserves it," his proud owner muses. "However, we are welcome regular visitors at the classic car meeting in Baden-Baden, probably the nicest rally in Europe, and we drive there under our own steam," Martin says, who is currently restoring a "Diamond Green" convertible with oval windows; he is also gradually putting together a 1302 and intends to restore a T1 van. Provided he is not cruising around in his 1958 Beetle, one of the first models with a rectangular window, albeit still the smaller version, or one of his classic Audi Quattros.

However, he wouldn't want to be without his split rear window Beetle. "Even just that special noise the exhaust makes thanks to the round tailpipe is like music to me. That's the distinctive, authentic Beetle sound. And nevertheless, the split rear window Beetle also has its own, unique charm." Even a decade buried beneath old tyres couldn't suppress it. ♥

Model VW Type 11C Export
Year of manufacture 1952
Location Rastatt
Country Germany
Owned by Martin Walter

A new layer of paint on the outside – this car is otherwise basically untouched.

W

Waldkirch / Germany

The barn find

A 19-year-old Beetle was taken off the road in the south-west of what was then West Germany in 1975 – and forgotten about for 36 years. The police actually became involved in its rescue! Not exactly with flashing blue lights, but by applying some detection skills.

Florian Ücker had heard that according to local legend, there was supposed to be an old Beetle stored in a barn somewhere. A really super car in insanely good original condition. Rumours like this are often sparked by a grain of the truth. Like a good wine, they become more full-bodied and richer as the years go by. This also applies to legends, somehow: more and more details are added and turn a grain of truth into a silo full of "facts". Florian was not blinded by these "facts", however, and realised straight away that there might be some truth behind the rumours after all when he saw an inconspicuous box number advertisement in the local paper: "1956 VW Beetle for sale to the highest bidder." It was impossible to glean more from this sparse information, but the policeman and Beetle fan realised at once that this could only be the

Florian Ücker is a policeman and therefore knows plenty of stories of drink drivers forced to leave their four-wheeled companions somewhere for a while. This particular companion was left for a very long time, matured into a classic and is now on the road again.

legendary oval rear window Beetle. Florian immediately launched a rescue mission.

The negotiations were extremely tough as other Beetle fans had also put two and two together and voiced their interest in the vehicle. According to the seller, there were ten seriously interested parties, even though the log book and the keys were missing and there was some accident damage, a reminder of a close encounter with a lorry. However, the lady who was selling it emphasised, what she did still have was the original sales contract from the Volkswagen dealership Büche & Tröndle in Lörrach. She added that the Beetle had only been driven 125,000 kilometres.

Florian charmed the elderly lady seller as soon as he met her for the first time. She particularly liked a postcard he showed her that pictured the two Beetles he had restored. "I'm in the running," he noted hopefully in his diary. "Advanced to pole position when I mentioned that I'm a policeman. Her husband was with the police, in Stuttgart, but is now retired..." – at this point in time, Florian Ücker had been with the service for 35 years and was based at Waldkirch station, where he belonged to the youth offending team. However, he had probably never imagined that his job would one day open the door to a secret barn. For the time being, though, he didn't even know where this secret barn was and certainly not how the little Beetle had got there in the first place.

Flashback. West Germany in the 1970s. Beetles were still a common sight on the roads. Although the Golf was starting to work the crowd, you could still hear that characteristic boxer sound wherever

PHOTOS MARKUS BOLSINGER   TEXT THOMAS IMHOF, BASTIAN FUHRMANN

This engine ran for the last time in 1975 and was then silent for many years.
It was covered in dust and wood shavings, as was the entire car.

This is what the barn find looks like today. The Beetle was carefully restored and now sports the cheerful historic colour scheme of a small local brewery. A happy second life after a long, long sleep.

you went. After all, Beetle drivers were no longer living life in the slow lane as the cute car with the rear-mounted engine was now available with up to 50 bhp. Admittedly, the improved performance made the ancestors from the split and oval rear window eras, which still had a long way to go until they were given classic status, looks rather bad: the geriatric boxers were scrapped by the score, a veritable insult to the cars that had been such loyal companions throughout Germany's "economic miracle" years. Quite a few survived, though, especially in rural areas where there are barns that are spacious enough to house hay waggons, ploughs, firewood for the winter and obsolete agricultural implements, and therefore also had room to spare for a little car. In any case, people who live in the countryside have a deep-seated aversion against wasting resources. Just throw a car on the scrapheap? No way. This had also been the case where this oval rear window Beetle from 1956 was concerned.

Master tailor Josef Thoma from Liel had originally treated himself to this car. The name of the small village in Baden-Württemberg's Lörrach district supposedly has Celtic roots and translates as "place where many vines grow." This still applies today as the area is well-known for producing good wine – and the master tailor, too, owned a small vineyard where the Beetle probably served him as a workhorse. To make it easier to transport the equipment he needed to look after his vineyard, tailor Thoma ripped out the back seat, and the little Beetle is likely to have been driven up the steep slopes and back down again with a heavy load and the suspension maxed out quite a few times in its life. In deep winter, which is the season when the vines are pruned, it was probably the safest mode of transport. In the autumn, when the first tasting of the latest vintage was on the agenda, it was likely to have been the driver rather than the vehicle that was loaded. At the time, drinking and driving was still not really considered an offence, and wine has always been considered a staple in scenic Baden. It was simply a different era. As locally rooted as its owner, the Beetle also never left Liel.

"I think Josef Thoma never made it beyond the district borders in his Beetle," its current owner reckons, who has spent a lot of time researching his car's history. It is therefore also obvious why the little oval rear window Beetle was suddenly taken off the road in 1975: the above mentioned lorry somehow got in its way. Repairing the damage seemed too much effort. That is why the barn became its home for a very, very long time. Mice scuttled between its axles, cats sharpened their claws on the increasingly brittle rubber seal around the charac-

Pure touring pleasure: **Florian Ücker particularly appreciates his Beetle's simplicity. A few flowers to liven things up, but no other decorations.**

teristic rear window whilst the seasons whistled through the cracks in the anything but airtight barn, and dust and husks gradually piled up on its roof and the front and rear bonnets. Layer upon layer, year after year: in the winter, snow tore through the timber walls; in the summer, the Beetle heard the birds twittering outside and, at most, maybe someone who was making hay or had a job to do inside the barn. Over time, such visits became increasingly rarer and the layer of dust increasingly thicker, until the windows disappeared completely and the story of the old Beetle that was put in a barn and waited for someone to rescue it simply became a local legend.

Until November 2011, when the barn door was suddenly thrown open, making the dust dance in the sudden burst of sunshine. Florian stood by the door, his shadow touching the little vehicle. For the Beetle collector, each step further inside the barn seemed like another step towards the past. He couldn't quite believe it yet. He was standing in the legendary barn. He was actually permitted to view the oval rear window Beetle; the lady had told him where to find it. Now they were standing inside that barn in Liel, Florian and his helper Miro Tuma. Of course, the Beetle didn't run and was seriously in need

of restoration; it had also started to rust in the typical places. However, the interior with the charming two-spoke Bakelite steering wheel and the flower vase didn't look too bad; he even found a magazine from 1974 in the boot. It didn't take them long to push the oval rear window Beetle out of the barn, and for the first time in many, many years, it saw some fresh air again. The windows were full of grime – but it seemed as if there was a hopeful gleam in the headlights, as if the car knew that better days were soon to come.

They started to thoroughly restore the find straight away; Miro Tuma – a close friend and a full-blooded technician – helped Florian to reawaken the Beetle with the oval rear window, and thanks to the efforts of many other people as well, the car came to life again. "Although the Beetle was in a surprisingly good condition when we pulled it out of the barn, we still gave it a thorough check-up. Of course, it had a few small things wrong with it."

The Volkswagen is now as good as new again, after a little bit of welding, some upholstery repairs, a technology overhaul and a new striking two-tone paint job. The design was inspired by a local brewery. "Very few oval rear window Beetles have survived, but if you do see one, they are often either black, green or the standard 'Polar Silver'," explains Florian, who finally decided on the shade of brown that the Hirsch brewery in Waldkirch has used ever since it was founded in 1868.

The design was modelled on pictures of historic brewery vehicles, and the rescued oval rear window Beetle now drives around with wings in a contrasting colour and the portrait of an impressive twelve pointer, the brand's logo, on the doors. We can safely assume that its wine-loving first owner would approve. Some people, after all, believe that the nicest thing about a glass of wine is the beer you wash it down with. ♥

Model VW Type 113 Export
Year of manufacture 1956
Location Waldkirch
Country Germany
Owned by Florian Ücker

P

Palm Springs / USA

A life beneath palm trees. The iconic cities of the US Beetle scene, Riverside and Anaheim, are not far away – Marlena leads a happy life in sunny California.

Marlena and the long distance relationship

Whenever he wants to see his Marlena, Chris Latshaw has to travel 1,200 kilometres to Palm Springs. She never visits him. Marlena's respiratory problems prevent her from driving to high altitude Durango.

We are shaped by our early childhood. Our subconscious memories of that time stay with us throughout our life. Like in Chris Latshaw's case, who was born in 1966. After his delivery in Portola Valley in California, his mother took him home in her "Tropical Green" Beetle. He then spent many years playing with the Corgi and Matchbox toy cars which his grandparents bought for him on their European travels – including some Beetles, of course. Maybe even the model which Grandpa 1 drove: "A white 1962 Beetle with tomato red interior," Chris recalls. Grandpa 2 worked for Pan Am and drove a smart Mercedes 280 SL – also a pretty cool car, but no Beetle.

Latshaw has been involved with cars in some way or another for most of his life and calls himself a "part-time car whisperer". At the age of sixteen, he had apparently not yet acquired the art of "whispering". Grandpa number 2 gave him a "terrible Ford Pinto" as a present that was in good nick and didn't have many kilometres on the clock. Not two years later, his former girlfriend reduced the Ford to a heap of rubble in an accident. Luckily no one got hurt, apart from the Pinto. The insurance company paid out 800 US dollars, and Chris's love affair with cars was rekindled. Back then, his mates all drove Toyota pickup trucks. Latshaw opted for a 1974 Super Beetle. Cost: 2,650 dollars. He knew full well that the Beetle was the cooler choice. More fun, lower fuel consumption and ideal for driving on snow. Latshaw still remembers a TV advert from 1963: "Have you ever asked yourself how the man that drives the snow plough actually gets to the snow plough?" The black and white TV spot shows a Beetle marching effortlessly through the snow. Snow was to feature heavily in Chris's life. He enrolled at the University of Oregon in Eugene, where the winters can be very cold and snowy. His chosen subject: political science – for no real reason. His interest in cars grew with every rally he went to. After university, he criss-crossed the northern USA as a service manager for various car dealers for a few years before he got fed up with the damp and cold weather. Driving a Beetle through the snow may be fun, thanks to the rear-mounted engine, but it harms the bodywork in the long term.

In Durango, he has long since found his perfect place: "It reminds me of how I grew up in California," he enthuses about the small town in the south-western most tip of Colorado. "We have 300 days of sunshine a year, and I am surrounded by the mountains. My current job leaves me more spare time that I spend with my girlfriend and our cars.

Chris Latshaw has always thought that Beetles are way cooler than pickup trucks. Marlena is his "second home Beetle". Instead of ploughing through the snow, she can bask in the Californian sunshine.

PHOTOS LISA LINKE   TEXT STACY SUAYA

Neither Chris nor Julie need the diagram on the gear lever, but they decided to leave it on the lotus white finish in a country dominated by automatic vehicles.

Isn't that what counts?" By the way, Chris insures almost anything in his latest job. Maybe also his nine cars. He has three Porsche 911s, a Cayenne, two M3s, a 1973 Sport Beetle and a Subaru Forester in his garage. His true love, however, a 1967 Beetle called "Marlena the Bug", lives far away from him in Palm Springs – his second home.

It happened like this: when he was searching for a 1977 fuel injection model – Durango is located at an altitude of almost 2,000 metres, respiratory distress in the form of carburettor problems would therefore be inevitable – he found the perfect VW online. The only snag: "The advertisement was four years old," he says, laughing. Chris nevertheless rang Randy Carlson, an overhauling specialist for classic VWs (oldbug.com). The '77 was gone, of course. He immediately focused on a model that was ten years older. "I realised that the true charm of the 1967 version lay in its unique design mix. Many parts were only used on the 1967 model. Enthusiasts revere the cars that were manufactured that year as the 'ultimate' Beetle." Unfortunately, Randy didn't have one. Latshaw continued with his search until he came across Eric Shoemaker (1967beetle.com), a 1967 model fan who had inherited his from his grandfather. Shoemaker knew where the

good ones could be found. "I know of a great car, but the guy who owns it is never going to sell it." Undeterred, Latshaw wrote an email to Mike Buettell.

The car was painted "Lotus White" and had a black interior – Chris was immediately smitten, even though Mike was already its third owner. However, the Beetle came from California and had never left the state – a good history. Mike knew what he had and roughly put it like this: "I'm not selling, but if I did, this would be the price." Astronomical! However, Chris wanted this Beetle. Clever as he is, he had the classic checked over by a friend who drew up an exacting list of defects. Their plan worked; Buettell reduced the horrendous price somewhat and wrote: "You seem like a nice guy, and you really want this car. I want it to go to a good home."

That evening, Latshaw and his girlfriend Julie drove to a gig by The Wallflowers. One of their songs, "Three Marlenas", happened to be on the radio. "Marlena the Beetle? A cool name." Google told them that it was an Austrian-German one. Its meaning: the matchmaker. Everything seemed to fit. His gut feeling was supported by the fact that once upon a time, the Beetle been restored by Virginia Coast Classic Restoration – a garage he had known since his teenage days. Latshaw bought Marlena.

Chris and Julie still live in Durango. "Marlena the Bug" is parked around 1,200 kilometres away in flat, sun-kissed Palm Springs – a city that, according to the statistics, even had 50 days more sunshine a year and thicker air for Marlena's carburettor. Both of them love spending time in the smart city in the Sonora desert that is populated mainly by pensioners. They like its style. Many houses are a Bauhaus interpretation of "mid-century modern" design. In the heat of the desert, they look cool, timeless and attractive – like Marlena when she travels along the roads of Palm Springs. ♥

Model Volkswagen 1300
Year of manufacture 1967
Location Palm Springs
Country USA
Owned by Chris Latshaw

A match made in heaven – Marlena is now a member of the family.

New beginnings in peacetime

Germany held its first international motor show (Internationale Automobil-Ausstellung, IAA) since before the Second World War in 1951. No longer in Berlin, as before the war, but for the first time in Frankfurt am Main. Although many of the visitors did not yet have enough money for a motor car, their enthusiasm and the audience numbers were huge. They particularly admired the Volkswagen models.

Volkswagen's cinematic stand design promised the big wide world. The lighting, mirrors and revolving stages turned the Beetle into the star of the show.

PHOTOS VOLKSWAGEN ARCHIVE | TEXT EBERHARD KITTLER

... N VOLKSWAGEN ALLE ZWEI MINUTEN
...GROSSE ERFOLG WERK UND WAGEN D...

The first IAA was held at the Hotel Bristol in Berlin in 1897. Eight motor cars were exhibited there and admired by only a few visitors. Those were the humble beginnings of the Internationale Automobil-Ausstellung (IAA), which soon became a firmly established event on Berlin's busy annual trade show agenda. The last show before the war was held in 1939. An incredible 825,000 visitors came to Berlin, above all to celebrate Volkswagen's new "Kraft durch Freude" car. The Second World War made sure that they didn't have anything much to celebrate for many years to come. After the war, it took a long time for a Europe that lay in rubble to pick up the pieces and return to normal life again. However, ultimately, unquenchable optimism and a sense of new beginnings won the day. Especially the reconciliation between France and Germany did much to promote European unity. It was also an era when an increasing number of people became interested in cars. Being able to travel meant getting on in life and represented progress.

The first IAA after the war began on 19 April 1951. However, it was no longer held in Berlin; Frankfurt am Main, which had recently missed out on becoming the new German capital by a narrow margin, was the ideal city to host the IAA. Unbelievably, the show attracted an amazing 570,000 visitors. Granted, most of them travelled there on foot, by bicycle or on the train – for most of the population, cars were still prohibitively expensive. However, the fascination for the motor car increased rapidly. It is therefore hardly surprising, considering the wide spectrum of models exhibited, that long queues formed at the gates hours before the show actually opened. The first President of the Federal Republic of West Germany, Theodor "Papa" Heuss, delivered the official opening speech. Interestingly, from today's perspective, the speech was not exactly a eulogy to the motor car, although it also left some contemporary listeners quite puzzled.

The eye-catcher at the 1951 stand was the Beetle produced for the Ethiopian emperor Haile Selassie in an opulent shade of mother-of-pearl with gold-plated and ivory details and a leopard skin covered interior. It was presented on a revolving mirror plate.

The IAA Frankfurt managed to attract around 500 exhibitors to the thirteen exhibition halls. Daimler and Ford each had their own dedicated hall. As did Volkswagen, although they already shared a hall with Porsche even back then. Wolfsburg and Stuttgart jointly presented their at the time still quite modest portfolio. However, Hall 2 certainly featured the most spectacular staging of the entire show. Today's visitors are still amazed by the imposing manufacturer displays at the IAA; the astonishment at the sight of the Volkswagen hall in 1951 is likely to have equalled theirs. Huge image boards and gigantic light arcs that spanned the whole stand and appeared to have cars driving on them were innovative as well as revolutionary. This entire landscape was masterminded by the film maker Franz Schroedter, who was also known as an imaginative set designer. Schroedter staged the Volkswagen models like icons at the show. This had never been done before, not least also because Volkswagen merely presented its Transporter van, simply called the Transporter Type 2, as a panel van, a so-called "Microbus" and a multi-functional cargo version called a "Kombi" alongside the Beetle. Admittedly, these models had already been launched before and merely featured some improvements on various details, for example: better ventilation, double doors on request and a large sunroof available for the Kombi and the Microbus. Stand companion Porsche didn't have many more innovations to offer: the 356 with a 1.1 litre engine and 40 bhp was basically yesterday's news. The only thing that was new was the more powerful 1.3 litre version with an amazing two (!!!) more bhp! Both were available as a coupe and as a convertible.

However, the other manufacturers weren't much better, really. Technical highlights were far and few in between. Borgward exhibited the first self-supporting car body as well as its 4-valve technology and an overhead camshaft. The turbo diesel was launched at the Frankfurt IAA in a Swedish lorry, and Daimler impressed those with an appreciation of technology with an electronically adjustable rear axle suspension.

However, none of this appears to have bothered the visitors who simply couldn't get enough of the glossy paint finishes, the chrome, the elegant designs. Volkswagens sold like hotcakes. Schroedter illustrated this with a huge illuminated sign by the stand that moved one digit every two minutes, because a new VW left the Wolfsburg production facilities every two minutes. In 1950, Volkswagen had managed to sell 90,558 vehicles. Only five years later, this figure jumped to one million. The enthusiasm for the brand could already be felt at the IAA, and they say that the Volkswagen hall probably attracted the highest number of visitors. Rumour has it that even the luxury cars produced by Daimler and BMW drew less attention. Of course, in hindsight, it is impossible to say whether it was actually the cars themselves that caught the audience's interest, or Volkswagen's revolutionary stand concept.

However, maybe it was also a very special Beetle Export model that was the crowd-puller. The mother-of-pearl coloured one-off mod-

The largely male audience inspects the details. New on Volkswagens: the additional vents in the side panels between the doors and the front wings.

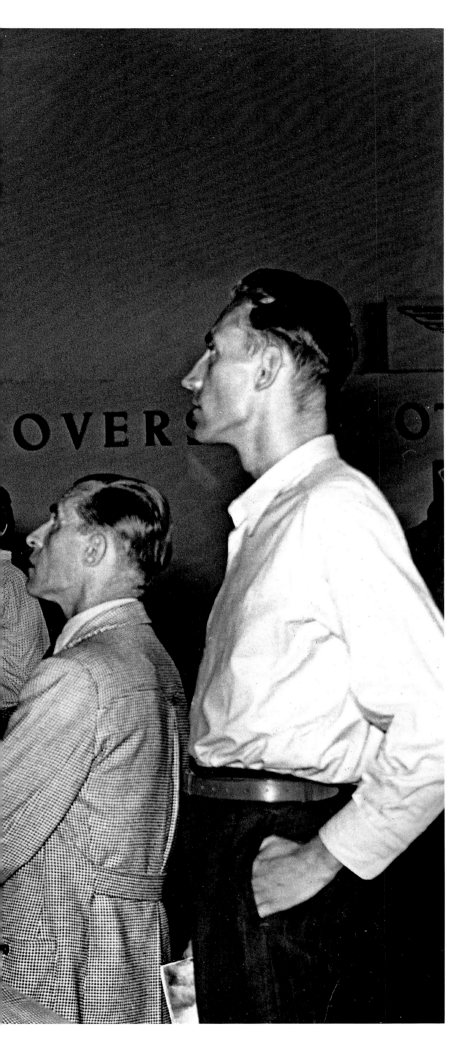

Oh, to own your own car! However, for the majority of the
population, a Volkswagen remained prohibitively expensive.
For the time being, the streets were ruled by people driving
old tricycles, substitute modes of transport and bicycles.

el built for the Ethiopian emperor Haile Selassie was displayed on a ro-
tating mirror glass pane. A "crotch cooler" model with rather unusual
"extras". In 1951, a custom job for an emperor looked like this: gold-plated and inlaid ivory details and a velvety soft leopard skin interior. Back
then, many of the visitors probably considered this car the epitome of
pure luxury. From today's perspective, it looks simply absurd.

Volkswagen's cheapest offer, on the other hand, brought many people back to reality with a bump. The entry-level Volkswagen cost
4,600 Deutschmarks. At the time, that was a simply inconceivable price
and roughly equalled one-and-a-half times the average annual salary. It
was the as yet unattainable goal people worked towards, and not only
in Germany. In 1951, Volkswagen already exported its cars to eighteen
markets and continued to vigorously pursue its export strategy. The company's vehicles were sold in the USA, some South-American countries
and Germany's neighbouring countries, for example, including the Saa-
rland, which belonged to France until 1955.

Film maker Franz Schroedter, on the other hand, ensured that ordi-
nary people identified with the brand's image and the sales figures suddenly leapt. He was not only the designer of the Volkswagen IAA stand
but above all also a documentary film maker, and in this capacity maybe the first to make a feature film length documentary about a car manufacturer. In 1954, he presented the VW corporate film *Aus eigener Kraft*,
which condensed the making of a Beetle down to a just over an hour and
documented the high quality of the brand. The film is now considered
a textbook example of a well-made documentary. Pride and pathos are
combined in striking black-and-white images with honest enthusiasm for
a peaceful goal. A new beginning for Volkswagen and a new beginning
in the Volkswagen, the classless motor car that mocks spirit quenching
totalitarianism with a democratic spirit. To this day. ♥

Playroom heroes

The cars are missing doors, the paint is peeling off, they have dents and are scratched, and all of them are reminders of times when someone spent happy hour after happy hour playing with them. If we look our heroes deep into their headlights, we might just hear a quiet "vroooom", "squeal" or "nee-naw" in a child's voice – sounds that are never quite forgotten. Christian Blanck captures this special form of Beetle Love in his affectionate pictures.

Car chase. A Corgi police Beetle chases its civilian counterpart, framed by two older Märklin Beetles. A yellow ADAC roadside assistance Beetle from Siku looks on. It's missing a door, but it has certainly brought someone many hours of fun.

Märklin close-up! However, the sensationally rare model is the one shown in the top right-hand corner: a metal Beetle from 1938, made by Nuremberg-based company Karl Bub. Our oldest hero.

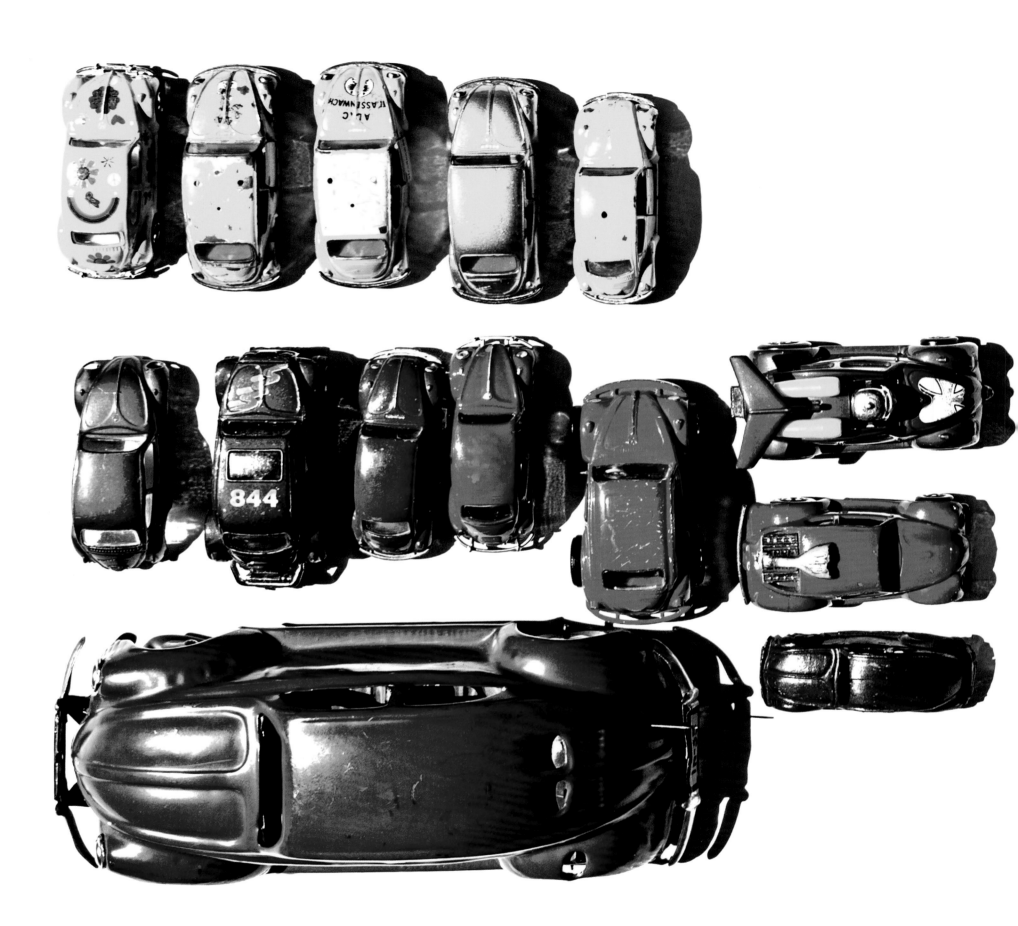

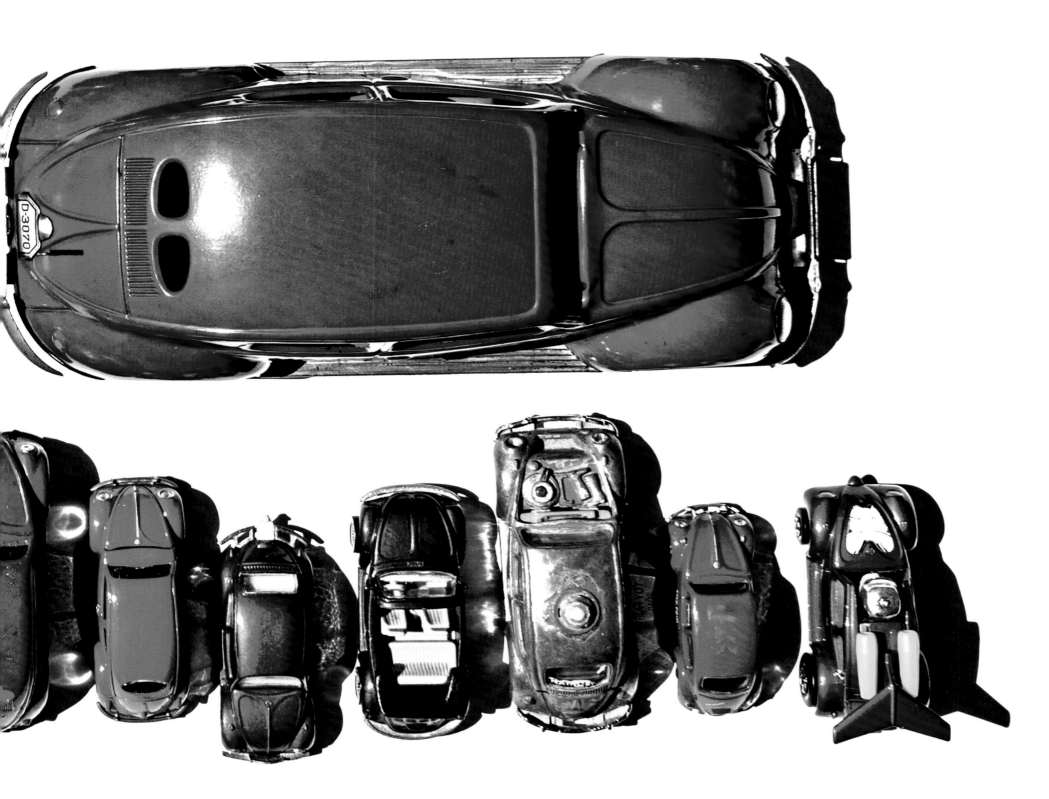

Fantastic diversity. Whether yellow hippie or red flying ace, cheap toy or a technology highlight like the red Diestler XXL split rear window Beetle facing towards the right. The model facing towards the left, by the way, is a Carrera precursor, a Beetle by Josef Neuhierl from Fürth (INF). Not yet a slot car, although it does have a slot for the engine controls.

W

Vienna / Austria – and the whole world

This Beetle has seen coastal dunes in the Western Sahara as well as Alpacas in landlocked Bolivia.

Globetrotters

Herbie is Super Bug. Sometimes, he is even part of a double act. Zainab and Dominikus Hocher are a super couple. Together, they went on a once-in-a-lifetime trip around the world. Over four years, they visited 80 countries on five continents with their Beetle – covering almost a quarter of a million kilometres. That's the thing with Beetles, they just keep on running...

Who hasn't sat on the sofa and dreamt, a globe on their lap that shows the big wide world in miniature? Turn it somewhat to the right or a little to the left; in your imagination, you are crossing the Equator. Oh, if you could actually do it all for real, really travel the world! A dream which ultimately, only very, very few people realise. "Why is that so?" thought Zainab and Dominikus Hocher: "Both of us are the kind of people who have always just wanted to up sticks and leave," is the disarmingly simple explanation Dominikus offers for their far-reaching decision. They spent four years on the road, visiting almost every corner of the globe. The young couple from Vienna clocked up a quarter million kilometres on its travels. What kind of vehicle should you put your trust in on such a trip? A car that literally just keeps on running, of course. Dominikus therefore decided that

they would travel not in an Unimog converted into a campervan or a Land Rover but in a Beetle, not least also because his experiences with the various Volkswagens he had owned over the years had always been good.

Beyond this, however, the couple planned very little. Of course they had to make some preparations; after all, you do need to organise visas for many countries in order to visit them. Even such mundane matters like a guaranteed fuel supply had to be sorted out beforehand as they also intended to travel to the most remote corners of the world, far off the well-trodden paths. As the Beetle which Dominikus had chosen for their journey around the world was white and had even been built in 1963, the obvious thing to do was to make it look a little bit like the famous "Herbie". This would turn out to have been an excellent idea on more than one occasion. The four-wheeled hero of several films is hugely popular all over the world. Other than that, they made few changes to the Beetle. The only really important addition was a tow bar as the two globetrotters intended to take their hotel along, a small, lightweight East German caravan originally built to be towed by a Trabant car.

They basically just left home – without any military-style planning down to the last detail, without any expedition equipment purchased from an online shop and above all, without the financial backing of a battalion of well-to-do sponsors. "We just read any travel warnings; apart from that, we just drove wherever we wanted to go," they recall. The first stage led them from Vienna via the Near and Middle East to Asia and then on to India. Their route: Austria, Hungary, Ro-

Dominikus and Zainab Hocher in front of the Mano del Desierto: In the middle of the Atacama desert in Chile, a hand reaches skywards, a work by the artist Mario Irarrázabal. It is almost six times as high as Herbie, but not as mobile as he is.

Real adventures, real backdrops. In Angola, Herbie and the QEK caravan were swallowed up by an Ilyushin, travelling in the hold; in Las Vegas, they discovered a miniature version of the Campanile di San Marco.

mania, Bulgaria, Turkey, Syria, Jordan, Saudi Arabia, United Arab Emirates, Oman, Iran, Pakistan, India, Malaysia, Thailand, Laos, Cambodia, Vietnam and back to India. In Chennai, they caught a ship to Australia. Once they had circled the fifth continent in its entirety, they boarded a ship again in Brisbane which took them all the way across the Pacific to Los Angeles. However, Zainab, Dominikus and Herbie did not cross the United States from coast to coast. In actual fact, they visited all 48 of the continental US federal states.

Next, the second stage of their agenda took them to Canada and Mexico, followed by Central America, from Guatemala and El Salvador to Honduras, Nicaragua and Costa Rica to Panama, then from there back to California. At that point, the trio had already been on the road for three years. Herbie desperately needed some well-deserved rest and recuperation. However, as the Austrian couple were still infected by the bug travel bug, they put the car in storage in California for the time being and acquired an almost identical one, Herbie II.

Next on their travel itinerary was a tour through Europe: Germany, the Czech Republic, Slovakia, Poland, Lithuania, Latvia, Estonia, Finland, Sweden, Norway, Denmark, the Netherlands, Belgium, France, the United Kingdom, Spain, Portugal, Monaco, Italy and Switzerland.

However, South America was still unexplored! So on the spur of a moment, they decided to reactivate Herbie I, who was still basking in the Californian sun. This time round, he carried the travelling couple via Mexico to Columbia aboard a ship from Veracruz. From there, they followed the Panamericana, not quite all the way to Tierra del Fuego but still quite some way through Chile and Argentina. Herbie and his crew crossed Ecuador, Peru, Bolivia, Paraguay, Brazil and Venezuela.

The only thing still missing, according to their agenda, was the fifth continent: Africa. Now it was Herbie II's turn again. From Vienna, they travelled via Genoa to Morocco and from there along Africa's western coastline all the way down to the Cape of Good Hope and then back up along the eastern coast. One of the biggest challenges for their outfit turned out to be coping with the infamous Trans East African Highway in Kenya during the rainy season. At the end of their trip, Zainab and Dominikus had finally also seen most of Africa: Western Sahara, Mauritania, Mali, Burkina Faso, Togo, Benin, Nigeria, Cameroon, Gabon, the Congo, Angola, Namibia, South Africa, Mozambique, Malawi, Tanzania, Kenya, Ethiopia, Sudan and Egypt.

Their journey around the world was almost complete. The couple had caused a stir in 90 countries on five continents and was able to look back on many wonderful experiences. The Herbie twins did

Off to the Andes. Bolivia was only a stopover on Herbie I's route from Mexico through essentially all of South America. His plucky single carburettor thoroughly appreciated the fresh mountain air.

Entel
BIENVENIDOS A BOLIVIA
WELCOME TO BOLIVIA
POLICIA NACIONAL
Bienvenidos a Bolivia
PARA EVITAR
53

Blue skies and seventh heaven. The glorious palm trees in Mozambique make you want to set off for Africa – and travelling around the world together makes you want to marry. The couple tied the knot in sunny California.

not let their passengers down even just once. The Hochers liked the USA best, not only because of its breathtaking camping options but also because of its many hidden gems, for example in California. They also have fond memories of Mexico. Its dream beaches and the exceptional friendliness of the people made a lasting impression on them. They also enjoyed South-East Asia very much, not to mention the policemen in various countries who did not stop the outfit to hand out penalty notices but only because they wanted to take a photo of Herbie and the two intrepid globetrotters. The many impressive pictures show how relaxed the couple looks despite the many miles of wear and tear on their bodies and the tyres. They are never pictured in full expedition gear or with an expression of dogged determination on their faces; instead, they are always wearing their everyday clothes and are in fact sometimes even dressed very smartly, and they beam happily at the camera. You can see that these two travel companions – sorry, three – got on really well. Of course, they experienced some stressful moments on their travels. Particularly the in part completely over the top bureaucracy drove the couple in the Beetle to distraction from time to time. They had to interrupt

their American tour, for example, because their passports were full to the brim with visas for countries and stamps, and the local embassy saw itself unable to issue them with new passports. Actually, the convoluted visa regulations for some countries, particularly in Africa, really tested their patience. A source of joy, on the other hand, were the special one-entry visas for country constellations with exclaves where you actually stay in the same country but have to pass through another country to reach the mother country's small scion. This applies to Cabinda, for example, a small exclave of Angola. To reach Angola, you would have to travel through the Congo. However, they did not have a visa for that country. The only option, therefore, was to travel by air. After a fortnight's toing and froing, the Angolan air force agreed to fly their outfit to the capital Luanda. Once on board of the gigantic Ilyushin freight plane, Zainab and Dominikus were permitted to sit in the cockpit, which compensated them for the tough negotiations. Being accompanied by extremely clingy military and police escorts wherever they went in Mali, Pakistan and Iran was not always a pleasant experience but important for their personal safety. The road conditions were sometimes also difficult, like on the stretch between Gabon and the Congo. The only connection between these two countries was a mud track with countless holes that are filled at least knee-deep with water during the rainy season. Herbie mastered these ponds armed with snow chains. Zainab waded barefoot through the water to find places that were shallow enough for them to cross. Are there any far-flung corners of the globe they would still like to explore? Oh yes! They haven't been to Alaska yet. Or to Russia. China. Japan. The North Cape. Antarctica. There's still such a lot to see! Also online, by the way! Follow their journey around the world at: www.herbiesworldtour.com.   ♥

Model Herbie
Year of manufacture 1963
Location Vienna
Country Austria
Owned by Dominikus Hocher

N

New York / USA

Not afraid of street canyons: Beetle
Gordy conquers Manhattan.

Beetles only! Round peg drives through square holes; every day with boxer-power.

Manhattan Transfer

Donald Morisette is a teacher at the Thomas Edison High School in New York. His students are often amazed to find a Beetle parked in their classroom from time to time.

"Gordy" lives in central Manhattan. His rent costs his owner about as much as a 70-square-metre apartment in one of the better parts of, say, Berlin. However, Donald Morisette doesn't care. The 37-year-old teacher at Thomas Edison High School in the New York district of Queens thinks that the six square metres in the multi-storey car park are just right for his Beetle, lovingly named Gordy. "He is well-guarded there and perfectly protected from the unpredictable weather here on the east coast of the USA," Morisette says.

Donald was only twelve years old when he fell for the Beetle. On his way to school, Donald and his mother had often driven past the weather-beaten little car from Wolfsburg which stood, forgotten about, in the front garden of a small house. "Sitting in the back of our car, I always noticed the curved silhouette out of the corner of my eye.

Donald Morisette fell in love with his Beetle "Gordy" as a teenager and earned the money to buy him by mowing other people's lawns. He became a teacher and now expands his students' repair skills with the aid of the Beetle built in Emden, Germany.

At some point, I made sure that we always went past there on my way home from school and from then on, I set my sights on it," the teacher enthusiastically recalls his own schooldays. "One day, I begged my mother to stop and asked around who owned the Beetle."

What followed were months and months of mowing other people's lawns. Donald had to earn the money for the Beetle himself, so for the time being, he just had first option on the Volkswagen. When he had finally saved up the total amount, they collected the Beetle and Donald and his father – who was just as much of a VW fan as he was – began to restore the vehicle from scratch at home. Whilst other boys went to baseball training, Donald spent his time fixing this curved vehicle his life now centred on.

Like in any emotional relationship, there were also low points which had to be overcome together. For example the time when Gordy was hit on the left-hand side by another car as it turned into a road on what was supposed to be Donald's last trip of the year before Gordy went into hibernation for the winter. The wings were seriously damaged and the frame was bent. Donald himself got off lightly. "I'll never forget that moment. We lived on an idyllic estate in New York with very little traffic. It happened in the last bend before the garage. Gordy was basically a total write-off, but my father, a few of his good VW friends and me got him fixed in the end, and he's till here today," Morisette says happily and leans against the open door of the friendly little Volkswagen.

"When I started to teach at this high school and a small lab was made available to us, the Beetle soon became the star of the school,"

PHOTOS THEODOR BARTH   TEXT BASTIAN FUHRMANN

Always on the road. The thin rimmed steering wheel in Donald's hands tells Gordy where to go. The padded dashboard proves that car manufacturers gradually developed an awareness of safety in the early 1970s. By the way, the small red light with the letter B on it is the dual-circuit brake system warning light. According to the manual, it indicates the failure of one brake circuit when the brakes are applied. Not a moment too early!

Fascinating study subject. Donald's students only have one question: Why did Volkswagen stop mounting the engine in the rear? Exactly. Why did they?

Donald says. Everyone was used to Cadillacs and Mustangs, so the appealing little car from Wolfsburg attracted attention straight away. The students at Thomas Edison High School come from very diverse ethnic backgrounds Maybe another reason why they welcomed the little German car with open arms. Unity makes you strong. That is the school credo.

"Despite the fact that Donald Trump grew up only five minutes away from here," adds Morisette with a wink. One of Morisette's Afro-American students, Aaron, is particularly interested in the Beetle. "Today, I am teaching them about the brakes and the suspension," explains Morisette. "The Beetle's technology is extremely simple, most of it is still easy to get to. Compare this to the Mustang over here," says Donald as a few interested students walk into the high school lab. "When did Volkswagen actually stop building Beetles with rear-mounted engines? It's a real shame they did," says Aaron.

Granted, Donald's Beetle is not always serviced by qualified professionals, but certainly with plenty of passion. "My students like to hone their skills on him, and Gordy patiently lets them get on with it," says Morisette, smiling as he gently pats Gordy's right wing. Gordy doesn't really look like he's been through the wars. The two of them have actually received an invitation to the Charity Concours d'Elegance. Word about Morisette's mechanical know-how even got out on the streets of Uganda. "On an adventure trip with my wife Amy, I repaired our vehicle a few times. At some point, I also fixed the broken down car of a local. The country has so many hidden treasures to offer, including many Beetles," Morisette says enthusiastically as he locks the doors to his high school lab and starts his journey back to Manhattan.

"The traffic in New York is sometimes absolutely diabolical. Constant stop and go. Gordy minds it less than I do." Tailgating these two through the traffic, several other huge American cars may well just squeeze their way in. However, the curved roof is easy to spot, even if you can't actually hear the growl of the boxer. Crossing the Brooklyn Bridge, the duo drives in zigzag lines, swerving to avoid the deep potholes in the dilapidated highway. The Hudson River flows calmly below them as they gradually leave the Big Apple's famous skyline behind. In front of them, hopefully many more wonderful and exciting road trips together.   ♥

Model **Type 11**
Year of manufacture **1970**
Location **New York**
Country **USA**
Owned by **Donald Morisette**

Quito / Ecuador

Head over heels with the round little car

Beetle fans don't come about by accident. Just like good beer: it doesn't just brew itself. Beer brewing is a skill you need to learn and dedicate your life to – and it calls for passion, preferably right from the start. Unless your name is Kimo Sanchez. He became one of the best beer brewers in Ecuador by accident. He also became a Beetle fan, again by accident.

The thing with Beetles is this: essentially, they will always get you there, no matter where "there" may be. That is why people love their Beetles. However, they do have allures sometimes and can get a little huffy. Like right now. Kimo Sanchez, 26, has put his car in first gear and slowly releases the clutch. The little car does absolutely nothing. An uphill start is generally not a problem for a Beetle, but this one seems to consider an uphill start on a mountain in Quito, the world's highest capital, a somewhat unreasonable demand. Quito is situated in the Andes at an altitude of 2,850 metres, and the cobbled alleyways of the historic city centre are so steep that they resemble a waterfall rather than a stream when it rains. That is why "El Fito", as Kimo calls his bright red Beetle, now lets its engine rattle in a pitiful way and is threatening to call it a day due to a lack of oxygen.

Kimo Sanchez is a chemist by profession. Perfectly qualified to brew beer, then. In Quito, the world's highest capital, his Beetle has to be able to climb. Although La Paz in Bolivia is actually situated even higher, it is only the seat of the government. Bolivia's capital is Sucre (at an elevation of 2,808 metres). Kimo is well-informed!

Kimo remains unmoved. He knows "El Fito" inside out, and he knows Quito. That is why, undaunted, he now puts his foot down on the gas pedal to give the Beetle no chance to give up. After all, Kimo is not just cruising around for fun. He is working. Kimo Sanchez brews craft beer (Kimo's Cerveza Artesanal), and his Beetle is his delivery vehicle. Boxes full of beer are piled on the back seat, and on the other side of the steep uphill rise, his customers are waiting: the trendiest bars on the Calle La Ronda, the hub of the historic city centre's nightlife.

It is Monday afternoon, and La Ronda is snoozing quietly away in the thin mountain air when the bright red "Vocho" parks up. "Vocho" is one of the many terms of endearment given to the Beetle in South America. It is pronounced "botscho" and is a sort of extremely mumbled version of "Volkswagen". Other names are "Pichirilo" or "Escarabajo"; both words for beetle in Spanish. Almost all Beetle owners give their cars a proper name. Kimo's is called "El Fito", because it reminds him of his older sister, who lives in Argentina. The reasons for this name choice are somewhat obtuse. It appears to have something to do with the fact that small, round cars are often called "Fititio" in Argentina, although this usually refers to a Fiat 500. Never mind, though, "El Fito" suits Kimo's car. Kimo winks and maintains a tactful silence when he is asked whether the name was inspired by associations of "small and round" with his sister.

Kimo started to brew his beer very early this the morning. He does this in the north of the city close to the Mitad del Mundo – a monument that marks the line of the Equator. Kimo's brewery is just a few blocks from there. It is actually a less-than-generously propor-

With the rear bonnet up to keep the car cool in the thin mountain air, this Volkswagen has been drafted in as a delivery vehicle. Well, the Beetle has always been and will always continue to be a workhorse at heart. Chévere!

tioned terraced house. Sacks full of grain are piled high in the bedroom. Hops and malt are stored in the kitchen and he brews, boils, cools and bottles his beer in the yard next to the washing machine. The label is attached in the living room and then everything goes into cardboard boxes.

Beer is Kimo's life, even though he doesn't actually like it much himself. He produces 2,100 bottles a month and makes seven varieties, one of which is fermented with cactus flowers. That is the only locally produced ingredient, apart from the fresh mountain water which comes out of the tap in Quito. "A shame, when you think about it," he says, "but we have everything else delivered from Belgium. Even the yeast. You can't get it here in the quality that I need."

Kimo became a brewer by accident, and unintentionally, along the way, also a Vocho fan. However, one thing at a time. Kimo is actually a chemical engineer, he has a diploma and everything, and his parents owned a restaurant in one of Ecuador's most romantic coastal towns called Mompiche – which has an endless beach, roads that are sand tracks, bamboo houses, and great waves for surfing. Everything is still quite un-

Can this be pure chance? Deep down, Kimo has probably always been a Beetle fan. "El Fito" is the bright red object of his affection. Heartache included.

spoilt. Tourists from the USA, Argentina, Australia and the rest of the world love it. The only thing they weren't happy with was the local beer. "Don't you have a craft beer here, something unusual?" they would ask Kimo's father.

So Kimo's father said to Kimo: "You're a chemical engineer, aren't you, surely you can brew beer, can't you?". In Ecuador, if your father asks you something like that in this way, you better just say yes. Kimo learnt what he could online, then he brewed his own beer. It was finished after 28 days, that is how long beer takes to brew, and people literally tore it out of his hands. Kimo brewed more beer, much more beer, and then opened a beer bar in Mompiche, on 24 December 2015. He closed it again on 5 January 2016. His beer had completely sold out!

He decided to move to Quito and to make the brewing of beer his profession. Chemical engineer is all well and good, but beer brewer is a cooler job, somehow. The brewing idea really took off. The only thing that was difficult was to actually deliver his product to the customers, because Kimo didn't own a car, only a trials motorbike. He would get on it with a box of beer squeezed between his thighs and drive off. Not a particularly promising or even scalable business model.

He needed a car. If you need a car, what you do is you ask around in the family, and sure enough, a cousin happened to be the president of the local Vocho club and had a pretty ingenious idea. "A Beetle," said the president, "is sexy, yet also frugal and affordable. We will buy a cheap one, do it up, sell it on for more and buy a practical pickup with the money we have made."

"Chévere", said Kimo, which means "cool", and then he and his cousin found "El Fito" online, who of course didn't know back then that this would be his name one day. El Fito was built in 1973 and cost 3,300 dollars (Ecuador abolished the Ecuadorian sucre a few years ago and adopted the US dollar as its currency). After doing it up, they would be able to sell it for twice as much money. Obviously, the boys from the Vocho club are pretty good at doing cars up.

However, then Kimo made a mistake. He got into the Beetle, turned the ignition key, put his foot on the gas pedal and heard the rear-mounted engine sputter and then come to life, raring to go. "That was the moment," Kimo now says, "when I fell head over heels in love. I realised that I wouldn't be able to part with the car for a while." Well, and now he's stuck with it, chugging through the city every day to deliver his beer to his customers. Unless something prevents him from doing so. Like high heeled shoes, for example.

That was a clear case of "being in the wrong place at the wrong time".The time was the last day of the year, and the place the street in Quito where "Viudas", young men dressed as women, let their hair down, literally. This is a nice tradition in a deeply Catholic country that usually makes life extremely difficult for transvestites, homosexuals and other members of the LGTB community. On New Year's Eve, they're allowed to really party. Unfortunately, Kimo and his car were

in the way.The "Viudas" simply walked across the Beetle in their high heels. After that, it took him a few days to get the dents out and to repaint the car.

These days, however, "El Fito" looks pretty fit.The repainted bonnet gleams in the sunshine. He is zooming across the six-lane urban motorway towards the city centre, overtaking all others. In Ecuador, there is no law regarding overtaking on the nearside and if there was, no one would keep to it.The traffic is anarchic; everyone just drives the way they want to. There are actually only three rules:

1: I don't care what happens behind me.

2: Don't get caught if you are doing more than the 100 km/h permitted outside built-up areas. If you do get caught, you'll spend two days in jail.

3: Learn your registration number off by heart and do not enter the city if the last digit of your number is on that day's "list", a system introduced to prevent the traffic coming to a complete standstill. If you do, your car will be impounded for three days.

Kimo keeps to all of these rules, and "El Fito" has behaved so well that he is allowed a trip up "the little bun" as a treat: a mountain in the middle of the historic old city centre that has an angel on the top and is called Panecillo, or little bun. The angel is huge and probably the ugliest angel of all times, a sort of fully tiled monster figure with wings, colourfully lit up from the inside. The Beetle happily pootles up the mountain; now that the beer has been delivered, it doesn't seem to mind going uphill. Kimo has arranged to meet a couple of his friends from the Vocho club at the top. Only one of his friends turns up, 39-year-old Belen with "La Nena", a beige 1979 Beetle made in Mexico. Unfortunately, the other friend couldn't make it. One of the tyres on his lowered roofless 1969 model died just as he started the climb.

Of course, this is not exactly a feather in the cap of his Vocho and puts paid to the claim that a Beetle always gets you there. However, who said that it has to get you there today? One day, the lowered, roofless 1969 will also make it to the top of the "little bun" and stand here, below the wings of the ugly angel, and all will be well again in the Beetle world. ♥

Model Type 11 (Mexico)
Year of manufacture 1973
Location Quito
Country Ecuador
Owned by Kimo Sanchez

H

Hamburg / Germany

Wallow in the mud! Erik's Beetles can and do!

Faithful companions to the limit

When Germany's Baltic Sea coast is being battered by the tides and the wind drives the salt and sand across the dunes, Erik Brandenburg is at his happiest. The man likes extremes, and his high legged off-road Beetles help him to constantly redefine his limits.

The vehicles that are parked in front of us will actually shortly be clinging to Ostholsten's steep sand dunes as effortlessly as if they were model cars arranged by children at breathtaking angles in a sand box landscape. The scale: 1:1. Although scale is relative. These extremely high Beetles don't fit the mould and do look oddly out of proportion. That doesn't matter, though, because their tall owner doesn't care a fig about the conventions. "The light weight of the Beetles is their decisive advantage out on the trail," 51-year-old doctor Erik Brandenburg shouts into the bitingly cold wind. "Each Volkswagen weighs a maximum of 730 kilograms," says the off-road rally fan, who has already taken part in the Africa Eco Race along original route of the Paris–Dakar Rally in an air cooled Porsche 911. After that, at the Transsyberia Rally, he even relegated almost all of the Porsche Cayennes

Erik Brandenburg is a Beetle fan. Rear-mounted engines are perfect for driving on heavy terrain, so his Beetles are mounted on VW 181 chassis as these are more stable and also higher.

that took part to the last places in his 911 Safari – simply because it has a rear-mounted engine. In the end, Brandenburg's luck nevertheless ran out: he could already see the finishing line when a raging river swallowed him and his 911. Increasingly, the doctor and passionate hunter not only relies on sports cars made in Zuffenhausen but also on air cooled models made in Wolfsburg. Beetles are just authentic. It is this authenticity that has made them the source of a completely new exhilarating driving experience for Erik Brandenburg.

However, this experience took some work. Erik had some very set ideas in his mind about what his Beetle would have to be like. High-flying ideas. An old friend helped him with the initial panel work – the Beetles were in a relatively desolate state when Brandenburg bought them. Gunter Wilken, formerly sheet metal worker at the VW factory in Poppenbüttel near Hamburg where he was the expert for amphibious and military vehicles, knows more about getting cars from the air cooled era into shape than almost anyone else. Wilken unbolted the Beetle bodies from their chassis and put them onto Type 181 Kubelwagen chassis, which was a lot of work as the floorpan halves had to be rewelded for this. However, an effort that was worth it because a Kubelwagen chassis has additional reinforcements at the front. You need those off-road.

To increase their ground clearance, Wilken welded some more sheet metal onto them and jacked the new hybrids up by eleven centimetres. No ramp, no slope is now too steep for them! As they were taken from 181s, the swing axles at the rear of each Beetle also en-

PHOTOS **ANATOL KOTTE**   TEXT **BASTIAN FUHRMANN**

Isn't this something of a sin? **To convert Beetles, and especially oval rear window Beetles, into off-road vehicles? Erik doesn't feel guilty at all. Of course it isn't a sin.**
Once you have been off-road with him, you are inclined to a agree.

sure an extremely short ratio between first and third gear. Another advantage: additional gears bolted onto the outside of the axle ends lift the centre of the axles above the centre of the wheels. Again, even higher ground clearance. Beetle drivers call this a gear reducer that acts like a small additional gearbox. Off-road drivers like Erik Brandenburg call them by their proper name, portal axles. In combination with a self locking differential, they turn the Beetles into off-road vehicles.

At the heart is a 1.8 litre engine with only 65 bhp. One might think that's rather too lame to be able to climb like that. "You don't need more." Brandenburg nips this fleeting thought in the bud. Drum brakes have been fitted at the rear, and at the front disc brakes from a 356 Porsche. An improved oil bath air cleaner protects the engine from any Baltic Sea or Sahara sand that might seep in. The exterior also leaves no doubt as to Doctor Brandenburg's safari intentions: a small spade has been attached to the right-hand side of the vehicle, and a thick rope to the left-hand side. The Wolfsburg desert kit is completed by two integrated winches on each vehicle. Former VW man Wilken, who misses the good old racing days and even qualified for the Ger-

man Rally Championship once, confirms that both Beetles have the perfect off-road properties: "These Beetles could easily take part in the next rally," he reckons. "Who knows, maybe I'll do the Panamericana next!", Brandenburg adds, laughing.

The doctor from northern Germany jumps into his favourite Beetle – known as "The Armadillo" – to warm up the rattling boxer engine. A glance at the engine cover reveals how the vehicle got its slightly odd name. The angled air vents obviously look very much like the scales on the plates of an armadillo. It was modelled on the casing of an emergency power supply unit used by the German army.

We jump into the other two Beetles, with the "Armadillo" in the lead. On the way to the area where he is permitted to hunt and practice his off-road skills, Erik suddenly steers towards a ditch on the side of the road and crosses it as if it didn't exist. A jaw-dropping sight. Brandenburg, on the other hand, opens his sunroof and shakes us out of our trance-like state. "What? Come on, what are you waiting for?", and the Beetles keep on rattling through the frozen brushwood. Erik is pulling us along on an invisible rope through the sparse landscape. We take every slope without difficulty and don't spill a single drop of the hot latte macchiato which Erik Brandenburg drinks several cups of every day.

We pass a huge fallen ash tree uprooted by a storm. Erik swings himself onto its trunk and points towards a nearby mountain. A mountain of earth with a gradient of around 60 per cent. Back into the Beetles. After a short run-up, Erik soon effortlessly climbs to the summit – forwards and backwards. Just for fun; just because his Beetles can. Incredible! Back at the yard, we are not only reluctant to say goodbye to Erik Brandenburg's Beetles but realise that we have actually fallen in love with them, just a little. For always.			♥

Model Off-road Beetles
Year of manufacture 2010–2013
Location Hamburg
Country Germany
Owned by Erik Brandenburg

A

Auckland / New Zealand – and the rest of the world

From kiwis to cookies

You travel once around the world in an airplane. Or in a Beetle. Like Ivan and Beth. They dared to drive from one end of the world to the other in a small Volkswagen. In 1961, the three of them just drove home – from England to New Zealand. As if that wasn't enough, 35 years later, the threesome repeated the tour.

Ivan and Beth Hodge were newly married. Their marriage was immediately put to the test as they had to spend some time in England for work-related reasons. From the Kiwi perspective, England is at the end of the world. Even though the concept of "end" shifted somewhat in 1961. Ever since Yuri Gagarin became the first human to fly into space, we know that viewed from above, "the world" just looks like a small blue ball. Viewed from the ground, however, Earth is actually quite vast, unexplored and unfamiliar, as Ivan and Beth would discover on their trips between continents.

The Hodges spent two years in London before it was time to return home. Getting onto the next plane was not an option for them. Instead of a plane ticket, they bought themselves a car. However, it had to be a vehicle that matched their personality. A small, austere car with charm. It had to be robust and easy to repair just in case something did go wrong along the way. Ivan decided it had to be a Beetle. New, blue, unassuming. A perfect match for his dainty wife, in his opinion. The German car already had an established reputation for reliability. The right-hand drive Beetle cost them 439 British pounds. Although the couple had already been married for around two years, they decided that this trip would be their honeymoon. A pretty cool honeymoon, not just from today's perspective. Also a financially ascetic one. The couple had a budget of just two pounds a day for themselves and the Beetle.

With their few belongings tied onto a roof rack, they left in August 1961. Besides maps and camping equipment, they also packed 72 tins of food in their almost standard Beetle. "We changed a few small details – like fitting reclining seats so we could sleep in it. And I sewed blue curtains for the windows," Beth recalls. A stopover in East Berlin was as obligatory as journeying on through the communist centre of Europe and the mysterious Near East with the Asian subcontinent as the ultimate destination. "We knew so little of the world back then," Ivan says. "That was before long-distance travel became popular. We really did drive into the unknown." They experienced one scary moment: "Around 18,000 kilometres on from London, we ran out of petrol in what was then known as the Persian desert. We had our refuelling stops meticulously worked out; I have no idea why we ran out of fuel regardless," Ivan says. "Luckily, we were found." The Beetle bravely soldiered on through Pakistan to Calcutta. From India, they caught a ship to New Zealand.

Beth and Ivan Hodges (in the background) chose to travel in a Beetle. On two pounds a day and with 72 tins of food on board, they left London for New Zealand in August 1961.

Adventure orient. **A fort in eastern Iran during their second long journey in 1996 and the Taj Mahal during the first, in 1961, when the Beetle was the only car parked in front of it.**

Once there, Ivan's father, a policeman, did his rounds in the frugal German car for the next twenty years. "Pub brawls would end the minute the distinctive shape of the Beetle appeared on the horizon," Ivan remembers. His mother died in 1996; she had kept the Beetle all those years right until she passed away. It was still roadworthy, but needed some cosmetic work. Thirty-five years after their honeymoon trip, Ivan had the idea to repeat the journey. In the same constellation. He had the '61 Beetle spruced up, and the three of them set off on honeymoon number two. A reaffirmation of their love for each other and an act of faith where the Beetle was concerned. "Our friends thought we were crazy," Beth says laughingly. They soon noticed that times have changed. "Our daughters insisted that we take a mobile and a laptop along."

Ivan and Beth enjoyed seeing how the various countries have changed and reflecting on how their own lives have changed since. The world has kept on turning and has become smaller. "On our last trip, we were naive, and it was a big adventure," Ivan says. "It was a much more intense experience this time round. The Beetle is the gooseberry in our marriage. It has been with us almost as long as we have been married."

The team has long since returned safely to the other end of the world. They now live in Australia, along with twelve grandchildren. The Beetle era had ended for good now – at least for these two octogenarians. "Our Beetle has travelled the world and has had an exciting life. That it might end up in a scrapyard one day was a terrible thought." A much better thought was to give it to the Museum of Transport and Technology (MOTAT) in Auckland. The museum knew the threesome and wanted the Beetle.

So they set off together one last time, returning to New Zealand. They were greeted by an armada of classic Volkswagens that escorted them straight to the MOTAT. "We feel honoured to have been chosen as Ivan and Beth's VW Beetle's retirement home. And we will make sure that their remarkable story isn't forgotten. This vehicle has become a symbol for tenacity, reliability, loyalty and innovation," said museum director Michael Frawley. Beth added: "It was incredibly emotional to go on a last trip together with the Beetle because it has played such a huge part in our lives."

Born in Germany, it was driven through Europe, the Near East and Asia. For most of its life, it has lived in New Zealand and Australia. The Beetle has managed to accompany Beth and Ivan through half a century, to make history and to forge links between wonderful people and fascinating places. With slightly over 300,000 kilometres on the clock, this Beetle has not just seen the world but also above all now earned a rest. ♥

Model Type 11
Year of manufacture 1961
Location Auckland
Country New Zealand
Owned by Beth and Ivan Hodges

Growing family: Beth and Ivan with their three daughters, their sons-in-law and their twelve grandchildren.

G
_____
Geesthacht / Germany

Harvest time

When a Beetle demands everything of the person struggling to rescue it, when its rescue means the world to two lovers, then the first outing in the car is so much more than just an enjoyable experience. It is the reward for something that has matured slowly but steadily, like seeds in the ground that ripen and finally flower.

Sascha Ahrens is certainly what you would call a genuine VW fan: moulded at an early age by his VW-owning ancestors, on the road at the tender age of eighteen in his own Beetle and always full of passion for the prototype made in Wolfsburg. Sascha admits: "Beetles are the love of my life." In love with the Love Bug. He doesn't mind admitting it as his wife Andrea shares his hobby; she's essentially part and parcel of the whole thing. She also shares his love for this oval rear window Beetle: "As lovely as the modern Beetles are to drive, we have always thought that these Volkswagens from the 1950s were much more beautiful. At some stage we realised, we simply had to own one."

For three years, the Ahrens family debated which Volkswagen model it was to be before they finally made their choice. Sascha then began to search for the right car all over Germany, which inevitably involved numerous disappointing moments, as well as wasted journeys amounting to countless kilometres: "I literally saw most of Germany during those three months. As well as twelve Beetles."

He finally found what he was looking for near Bielefeld, although in conditions that were anything but promising for a classic Beetle; the oval rear window model they had dreamt of and searched for so hard stood in a wet barn extension, of all places. It was not so much a garage but more of a tomb. The car they found there in the damp rotting away on brittle tyres was in a truly sad state – it didn't even have the right engine anymore. "The Beetle looked absolutely terrible. More rust than paint and holes everywhere!"

If cars could cry, this early oval rear window model certainly would have bemoaned its fate: "The interior lining hung down in shreds, and on the front left-hand side, it also had some accident damage. What can I say: I bought the Beetle, in the end, simply because I felt sorry for it." Sascha shrugs. He casts a melancholic sidelong glance at his oval rear window Beetle. There it is again. The lump in the throat, the pull at the heartstrings. Just remembering the state the love of his life was in when he found it still makes him feel as anguished as on the day they met, when he first beheld the dismal scene.

However, then and now, his anguished expression soon gives way to a smile like a ray of sunshine on the horizon. Sascha saw beyond the terrible rotten state of the car, but he also saw that it had potential. "I knew I could turn it around." Sascha is a vehicle technician, so he knew he had the necessary skills. The Beetle nevertheless still

Andrea and Sascha Ahrens like classic Beetles. Granted, the newer models might be more comfortable to drive – particularly the 1302 and the 1303, but you only get that authentic feeling with shoulder bolts and an irrepressible 24.5 bhp.

PHOTOS JAN BÜRGERMEISTER   TEXT HEIKO P. WACKER

had some surprises in store for him, too. "And how!", it was almost as if the little car had intentionally hidden the worst of its infirmities; understandably so, it probably just wanted to escape its damp tomb at all costs.

The whole extent of the damage was revealed when he took the car apart. "Lots of parts were missing, and the interior was totally moth-eaten. The VW also had a bent axle thanks to the accident and a broken side panel." This wasn't something he could attempt to fix without professional help, as the Ahrens family wanted to restore the vehicle back to its perfect original condition.

The early oval rear window models didn't have a 30 bhp engine fitted, for example, they still featured the original split rear window Beetle motor, which had a modest 24.5 bhp. The engine in this Beetle was obviously a much later 34 bhp one. It had to be replaced with a matching boxer engine with the correct 24.5 bhp, which again meant a long search. "I found one owned by an elderly gentleman in the Rhön Mountains who had put it by as a spare for his Kubelwagen."

The engine wasn't the only problem, though, considering that the hero of this story is an unusually early model, even for an early oval rear window Beetle, as it still features quite a bit of the split rear window model technology, despite the fact that its rear window is already curved in the more modern way and not split in two. "That is also why we wondered at some point whether we hadn't taken on too much. Never in a million years had we imaged

Batman rides again! The two spoke steering wheel with its "bat wings" is typical for the models from this era. Very few accessories adorn the beautifully austere metal.

just how much blood, sweat and tears and also money this car would ultimately cost us. We simply stopped counting the hours we invested in it." Today, all of these efforts are not quite forgotten but have at least been forgiven. What has remained is a rather unflattering nickname: Dracula. "Suits him, doesn't it?", Sascha says with a grin. The Beetle doesn't seem to mind. Dracula? Pfft! At least it is now standing in a cornfield in the bright sunshine and pays them back every ounce of the strength the restoration has cost – or rather, the car borrowed – with every kilometre.

After all, it is not the car's fault that the brakes and axle parts had to be elaborately sandblasted, galvanised or painted before the floorpan could be put together again. However, seeing what rests on it – the cab – finally shine freshly repainted in the original colour, "L41 Black", was a heart-warming sight to behold. The time had come for the almost finished Beetle to go on its first trip, from the paint shop back home to his garage. Sascha transported the car himself in style, with a vintage tractor as the towing vehicle: "I drove my Deutz four hours right across Schleswig-Holstein with the floorpan on a trailer." Once the cab had been "reunited" with the floorpan, he returned home again that same day – another four

Sascha looked at a dozen Beetles. He did not chose this one because of its condition, which was truly deplorable back then, but because it was the model he and his wife were looking for.

Fun on the road. Andrea loves their outings in the Beetle. And her Sascha, who is seen here flying heroically across a stubble field. A lot of work has gone into this Beetle, but it was worth it!

hour drive. Next, they tackled the upholstery and the interior trimmings – final assembly! After almost six years of restoration work, getting the "vehicle of historic interest" certificate was a pure formality. Dracula also really has a history now: "Whenever I had some spare time, I did some research on its history and previous owners. And I found out almost everything there is to know," Sascha says proudly. "I even managed to get a picture from 1954; it was given to me by a grandson of the first owner."

Telling the whole history would fill a whole book; to keep it short: "The car was built on 3 October 1953; two days later, it was in a showroom in Mannheim – where it was immediately bought by an architect," Sascha Ahrens says. Later on, the Volkswagen was on the road for some years in the small town of Reilingen, only twenty kilometres away from Heidelberg. Sascha was able to trace all of its previous owners and managed to contact many of them. The car was used as an everyday

runaround until the 1980s and finally ended up with a fan – who then inexplicably left it to rot outdoors. The oval rear window Beetle, by now covered in moss and adhesive tape to vaguely protect it from water ingress, was not sold to its Bielefeld owner until the late 1990s, where it then proceeded to mould away in the above mentioned barn, its damp tomb for many years.

"The previous owner had actually planned to mount the cab onto a modern floorpan. Luckily, he didn't have the time so the Beetle stood there on its increasingly flat tyres – until I came along. And I could swear that the little car gave me a grateful wink with its headlights when I freed it from that damp hellhole." A trick of the imagination? Probably not!

When Sascha found the Beetle, he had no idea just how rare it was. "They built this particular Beetle model for only one year; it is almost identical to the split rear window Beetle – in fact, the only difference lies in the window design. I didn't know it back then, but it would be precisely this fact that would cost me a lot of money and nerves. Finding the right parts or even just reliable information was fiendishly difficult. But it was worth the effort."

He now uses the rare early oval rear window Beetle as it should be used: "We cruise through Hamburg or drive to one of the lakes in the nearby countryside, that's what we enjoy most." As he speaks, Sascha Ahrens gently strokes the curved roof that was covered in moss only a few years ago. "Well, quite a successful rebirth, I'd say." ♥

Model VW Type 11C Export
Year of manufacture 1953
Location Geesthacht
Country Germany
Owned by Sascha Ahrens

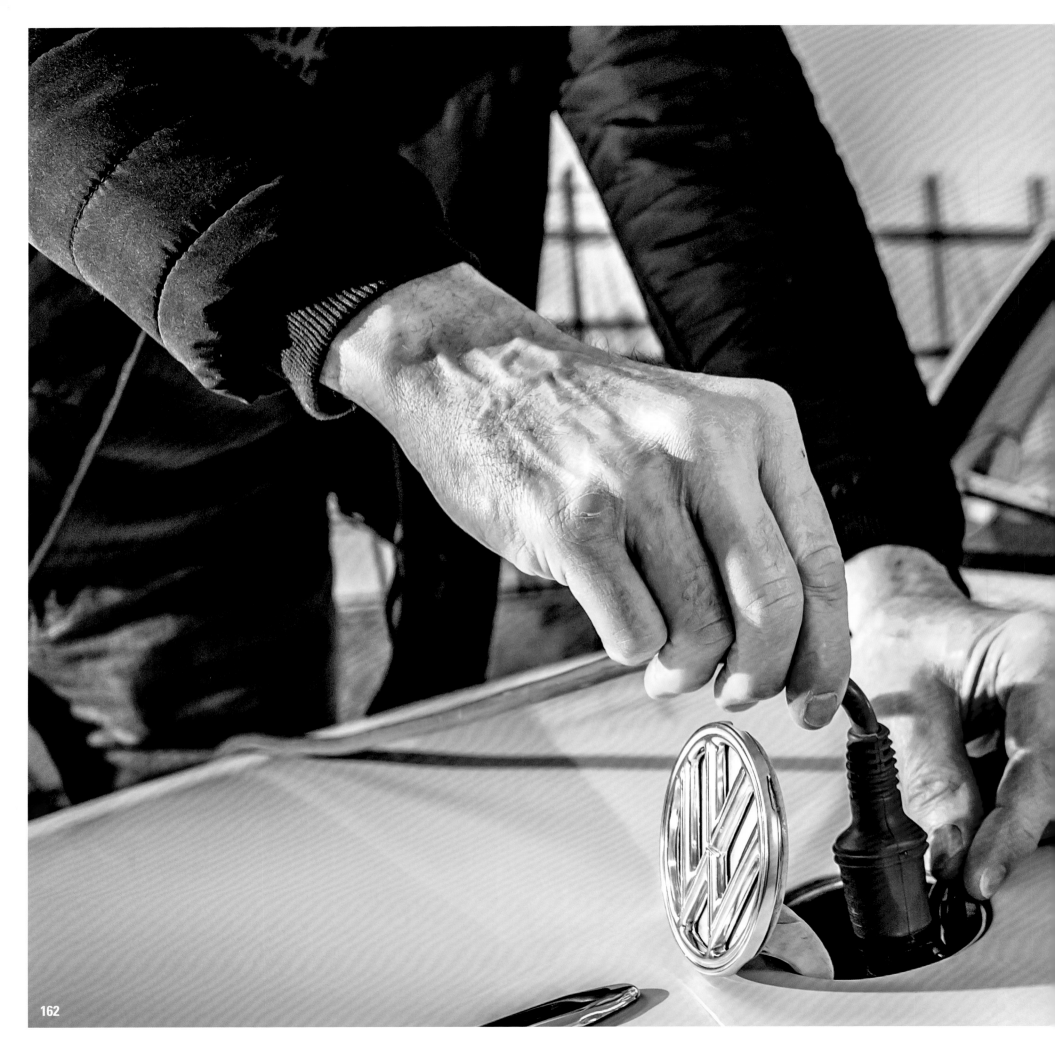

G

Gelsenkirchen / Germany

The heart of a boxer

Something seems wrong here...but what? Wolfgang Doetsch glides past in his 1957 oval rear window Volkswagen Beetle. Only after he is long gone, you realise: what is missing is the typical sound of the boxer engine. All you can hear is an electric hum.

"I can charge my Beetle conveniently at home in my garage. Overnight, just like that," Wolfgang Doetsch says and flips down the Volkswagen badge on the front of the bonnet. A small charging socket has been fitted inside the circular hole. He plugs a green cable into it. All he has to do now is wait. However, the inventor, who actually earns his living as a fire safety engineer, doesn't mind: "I want to drive a Beetle, but without the noise, without the oil stains, without harmful emissions," Wolfgang Doetsch clearly states his mission. "Finished!" he adds, with a slight accent that betrays his roots in Germany's Ruhr region (he is also a dedicated fan of local football club FC Schalke). The "Beetle fan from birth", as he calls himself, tends to speak plainly. That is also why he is not bothered by the fact that some purists disapprove of him and his Beetle at VW rallies. They seem to almost consider it a sacrilege

Wolfgang Doetsch is forward-looking, even though he is actually looking backwards in this picture. He is an electric transport pioneer. His Beetle is a highly charged model, which sometimes causes quite a bit of confusion.

that Wolfgang has removed the one thing that defines the Beetle, apart from its shape. The friendly growl of this engine has sent millions of happy little children to sleep on the back seat. The sound a Beetle makes is absolutely unique. However, he would have put an end to the friendly growl, anyway. Originally, he was aiming for a greedy roar, rather than a discreet whisper.

When Wolfgang bought the 1957 Beetle in 1989, its life was actually as good as over. The ravages of time had corroded the formerly solid body until it was hardly more than a collection of rust holes painstakingly held together by the remaining bolts, some filler and a bit of wire. Wolfgang's plan: to restore the oval rear window Beetle, to make it more lightweight all over, to whack a 2.7 litre boxer engine into its rear and to then take part in drag races, which were the latest craze back then. Racing fans would meet on airfields abandoned by the Allied forces to compete against each other across distances such as an eighth of a mile or a quarter mile. However, building a house and starting a family changed his plans. Initially, the project car just stood around on increasingly flattery tyres before he finally turned the monster dragster into an eco hero. The low weight of the Beetle, it weighs a mere 700 kilograms, inspired a totally different concept: "I couldn't seem to let go of the idea of building an electric car," Wolfgang Doetsch recalls. One day, he simply began.

Nothing is off the shelf on this Beetle. However, not so as you'd notice. The electronic control system instruments are hidden behind the flap that usually covers the slot for a radio. The large grill for the mono speaker now houses a modern radio with

PHOTOS THEODOR BARTH, ANDREAS LINDLAHR   TEXT THORSTEN ELBRIGMANN

Kiosk meetup. This oval rear window Beetle was once destined to become a dragster. A monster car like that would have frightened little children away; now they approach it with the utmost curiosity.

concealed integrated speakers. Wolfgang Doetsch opens the very much lighter driver's door and sits down on a sports seat that rests on an aluminium frame. The floor plates underneath? Carbon fibre composite panels. Front and rear bonnet and wings? Glass-fibre reinforced polymer. The windows? Makrolon polycarbonate – as used on racing cars. The effort that has gone into every detail is completely invisible. The ignition key turns in the original lock on the dashboard. The only noise you can hear is a low hum. Wolfgang Doetsch checks the control lights behind the radio cover, nods with satisfaction, closes the cover and reverses the car out of the garage. You can hear the wheels grind on the gravel below. The 85 bhp rear-mounted engine is quieter than the rustling of leaves moved by a gentle wind. Wolfgang has to move off in third gear. Otherwise, the 390 Nm torque would tear the ancient gearbox apart. The Beetle makes a powerful leap forward. The only noise is the screaming of the gearbox. Apart from that, silence. A passer-by smiles when he sees the Beetle. Then he frowns. The electric car fan looks into the rear view mirror and smiles: "He's got it now."

People often approach him as he parks up, either because they have seen him and his Beetle around before or because they spontaneously notice that the little white car is so amazingly quiet. Wolfgang Doetsch patiently explains everything. Electricity powered

His owner's pride and joy – passers-by are usually amazed: **its rear bonnet hides a high torque electric motor. Its range may be short, but the fun factor is huge!**

transport, coupled with the aesthetics of a classic car – people are fascinated. However, as nice as the new world of zero-emission local transport may be: it also has its downsides.

Wolfgang likes to use his electric Beetle to commute. He can even cover the distance of six kilometres there and back several times on one charge: "However, I can't manage more than 40 or 50 kilometres in one go, at the most." That is due to the batteries. The lead gel batteries that are distributed all over the car weigh 270 kilograms. They don't pose a problem in thermal terms as they do not have to be cooled like modern lithium polymer batteries, for example, or lithium iron phosphate batteries. Lithium cells also require far more complex electronic controls. Wolfgang just has to connect the batteries for his lead gel Beetle to a 220V socket for three to four hours – and he is ready to roll, albeit

across a relatively short distance. By the way, the engine comes from a mineral tramway and the controls from a forklift truck. If need be, all components are quick and easy to replace. The spare parts availability is also good.

Wolfgang Doetsch nurtures a very special kind of Beetle Love. Due to the dragster conversion, the lotus white car would never have got "vehicle of historic interest" approval in Germany. However, because it is an electric vehicle, low emission zones aren't an issue; it can therefore be used like any normal car. The perfect second car, when you think about it – provided you can live without a heating system, which the Beetle hasn't got: enough range for doing the shopping, incredibly cheap to run – and also incredibly cool. Not surprising, then, that companies like "Classic eCars", which is based in Hilden in Germany, and other firms have specialised on converting classic cars to electric. The Hilden experts also helped Wolfgang with his conversion, which, incidentally, he has never regretted: "Due to my dragster plans back in 1989, it wouldn't have been possible to restore the care to its original condition, anyway. And I think that my electric Beetle showcases how amazingly versatile these old Volkswagens are. Even today." ♥

Model **Electric Beetle**
Year of manufacture **1957**
Location **Gelsenkirchen**
Country **Germany**
Owned by **Wolfgang Doetsch**

U

Ulfborg / Denmark

Trip down Memory Lane

Denmark's west coast seems to be located in a very special time zone. One that makes you believe what was already good yesterday's is sometimes still the best today. Especially on Sundays. That's when the museum run by Sussi and Carsten is open to the public.

Sussi and Carsten met in 1988. Carsten left Sussi waiting for an hour at a petrol station – which he happened to own. Unfortunately, he had gone to somewhere in the middle of nowhere to look at a classic car together with a friend who was interested in buying it. At this point, at the latest, Sussi probably realised that his priorities differed somewhat from those of "normal" Danes. Nevertheless, Carsten and Sussi are now happily married. Sussi has long since forgiven him for that wasted hour of her life.

The Andersens love the past yet also have both feet planted firmly in the Here and Now. With their VW & Retro Museum in Ulfborg, they prove that the faded past and the colourful present can look amazing together. Ulfborg, population 2,000, lies on the west coast of mainland Denmark, around 400 kilometres away from Hamburg in Germany. Not too close to anywhere, really, neither to Wolfsburg nor to the rest of the world. Yet both of them thought it would be a good idea to open a small museum there that celebrates the beautiful design of the era from the 1950s to the 1970s. Wherever they look, visitors are greeted by the friendly face of the VW marque.

The unadorned industrial hall, which measures around 2,000 square metres, is the perfect setting for Carsten's collection of shiny Volkswagens. Only the words "Team Andersen" above the entrance hint at the fact that the inside might have more to offer than the outside promises. His core "team" consists of a T1 Westfalia and a pickup, a Type 3 TL, four Beetles and a Mk 1 Golf. They are joined by some "odd men out", such as a Karmann Ghia or a Formula Vee racer with a Beetle engine, gearbox and suspension. Carsten pours all his love for anything with an engine into these treasures, their technology as well as their looks.

A van built in 1967 is the latest vehicle he has restored from scratch. Its previous owner was a furniture maker who used it to deliver his furniture to his customers. However, the furniture maker also ran a funeral parlour. An old photo on the wall supplies the proof. It shows the pickup with the drop down sides down to reveal the respective, considerately worded information. Sides folded down = hearse. Sides folded up = furniture transporter. A very economical approach. Sadly, we do not know whether the light brown coffin shown on the photo was also produced in the owner's joinery workshop. However, Carsten has many such stories to tell and loves to regale his visitors with them.

Carsten Andersen and his wife have set up a wonderful Volkswagen museum. When he sits in his T1 van with the Westfalia awning, it feels the authentic camping experience – albeit underneath a hall roof, rather than the open skies.

PHOTOS STEPHAN LINDLOFF   TEXT MARTIN SANTORO

Shiny relics of a bygone age. The Beetle Export model stands facing the T1 van (mirror on the right-hand side) and a red VW 1600 TL Fastback.
A small boy walks his fox terrier; a Golf is lurking in the background.

He is particularly proud of his 1963 T1 campervan. Not surprising, considering that this is an SO36 Westfalia with original interior fittings. It is even equipped with a washbasin that fits snugly into the door pocket – and is also home to the more than 100 trophies which the camper has garnered at rallies so far. The Andersens also holiday in the van; the couple has travelled more than 80,000 kilometres in the V-Dub. It was the second vehicle Carsten restored. His first restoration was a 1303 "Olympic Blue" convertible. Appropriately, this Californian import was intended for Sussi. That was back in 2003 and probably provided the initial spark for what was to come.

Carsten has always been interested in cars, ever since childhood. A passion he inherited from his father – as is so often the case. His father owned the above mentioned petrol station, which he acquired in 1957. He expanded the business by importing Massey Ferguson tractors to Denmark from the USA. In the 1960s, he also started to sell Volkswagens on the Danish North Sea coast. Carsten was always with him – at the petrol station and in the showroom. He was basically born loving Volkswagens. He learnt to drive in a Mk 1 Golf; the first car he actually owned himself was also a Mk 1 Golf. He now has one on display in his museum. A rather bright green model

from 1977. The car was imported from Sweden, unrestored and in immaculate original condition.

The couple had toyed with the idea of opening a "VW & Retro Museum" for quite a while. One thing they agreed on straight away: it would focus on more than just one theme. Sussi obviously also loves VWs. However, a tour of the museum shows what the lady of the house also likes: all kinds of beautiful vintage knick-knacks – provided they are well-made. From clothes to furniture and accessories from the 1950s through to the 1970s, she collects everything that other people often just want to get rid of. Some people might call her a nostalgic. Most, however, would agree that she has good taste. The attractive way in which the exhibits are displayed in the museum is therefore mainly her work. They offer subtle proof of the typical Danish flair for design; even here, a long way away from trendy Copenhagen. Sussi has arranged the small objects on shelves and in glass-fronted cabinets; many of these serve to cleverly set the stage for the actual exhibits, for example the 1950s picnic set displayed in and around the Westfalia VW T1 or a traditional Danish corner shop that has been integrated into the museum in its entirety. The museum conglomerate also includes the almost fully equipped spare parts store of an old 1970s VW repair shop.

Just in case you were wondering why the VW & Retro Museum is only open on Sundays, the reasons for this are obvious: during the week, Carsten clocks up 60 hours as a lorry driver these days and Sussi works as a measurement and control technician for speaker manufacturers Bang & Olufsen. They spend most Saturdays focusing on new additions to the museum – in some way or another. Their latest acquisition is an orange T2 crew cab pickup – from freezing Greenland. They intend to start restoring it over the winter – how apt. Sundays, however, are museum days. That's when things get cosy, with freshly brewed coffee, homemade cake and lots of love.   ♥

Model Numerous Volkswagens
Year of manufacture 1950s to 1970s
Location Ulfborg
Country Denmark
Owned by Sussi and
Carsten Andersen

J

Jember / Indonesia

He's part of the family

Jakarta. Thirty million people live in and around this metropolis. Ten million of them in the city, which isn't actually a city officially but a province. Although everything is very urban and impersonal, family is still the most important thing for almost all of its inhabitants, including the Waluyos, a Beetle-owing family since 1962.

Jakarta is a high-tech hub and is growing at an alarming rate, accompanied by everything such rapid growth entails: rampant consumerism and poverty, happiness and suffering, chaos, heat and noise. However, like in all megacities, there are also countermovements. People who live life at a slower pace, who manage to carve out green oases for themselves in the middle of all the hustle and bustle. People who love vintage things. These things are often analogue, handmade, of outstanding quality and above all durable.

For example, there is a large community of denim fans in Indonesia. Not just any old denims but dark blue jeans made from heavy denim that is produced on old, narrow looms. Made in Indonesia, of course. For the past few years, young, quality-conscious Indonesians have copied what is rarely manu-

factured in the USA these days and what the Japanese can make much better than the Americans by now, anyway, and they have been internationally successful with this. These jeans are expensive yet still worth the money. From the buyer perspective, it makes financial sense to resist the overwhelming variety of clothes available. They simply wear a pair of jeans for as long as it lasts.

Italian scooters have even more fans. The Vespa craze is more widespread in Indonesia than anywhere else in the world. Of course, they must be original classic models from the 1960s and 70s. In this country with 260 million inhabitants, many people revere Vespas almost religiously. Well, all Indonesians are actually required to have a religion, by law. Islam is the religion of choice for 200 million of them; many of these Muslims are also "Vespisti" – as Vespa riders call themselves with pride. They will ride their Vespa until it falls apart.

However, Indonesians also have a passion for something else: classic VWs. Kubelwagen military vehicles, vans and above all Beetles were once extremely fashionable in this country, which is made up of around 17,500 islands (6,000 of which are inhabited). Yoyok Waluyo has also loved this German car marque for what feels like an eternity.

This eternity actually began in 1962, when his great-uncle bought an eggshell coloured Beetle ("Pearl White", L87) from a local Volkswagen dealer. A right-hand drive model, which is still the norm in Indonesia. Twelve years later, the uncle sold the Beetle to Yoyok's father, for a nominal sum – he just wanted to make sure the car went to a good home. As family matters were as important back then as they are now, it was a given that Yoyok's father would look after the Beetle

Yoyok Waluyo has known this 1962 Export model all his life. His great-uncle bought it initially and then passed it on within the family. Now it's Yoyok's turn to look after this family heirloom.

and take good care of it. It was also the first car than Yoyok's father actually owned – he was extremely proud of this fact – and as a small boy, Yoyok would often accompany him on his trips through Jember, which lies around 1,000 kilometres to the east of Jakarta.

In 1983, the Beetle was passed on, although it was always kept in the family, of course. Another four relatives enjoyed the reliable German car before it was Yoyok's turn in 2017. Obviously, the Beetle had suffered some dents and scuffs in the course of more than five decades – not unlike the eldest Waluyo son.

Although Yoyok has some DIY skills, he decided to employ a professional when it came to giving this sacred family heirloom a facelift. This professional is called Rolly Sanger, and he is one of the best-known VW revivors in south Jakarta. Sanger has his own repair shop and repainted the 1962 Beetle in the original colour; he also cleverly refreshed the interior. In the course of the restoration,

he also replaced the original (1200cc) engine with a 1500cc version with 44 bhp, which means it now also has enough juice to power an air conditioning unit. Not a bad idea, as the average temperature in Jakarta, where the Beetle is mostly driven, is 27 degrees Celsius – all year round. When you drive a car, your T-shirt will stick to you faster than the flies to the windscreen. Come to think of it, this is a rather inappropriate comparison, as in Jakarta, cars spend more time standing in traffic jams than actually moving. There is no airflow.

Yoyok has long since joined the Volkswagen Beetle Club Jakarta, where his story of lifelong family-ownership is still one of the more unusual ones. He proudly shows his immaculately restored 1962 model at VW rallies and loves to talk petrolhead talk with the amazed visitors. Two photographs that Yoyok always carries with him never fail to make people smile. One photo shows a house, the Beetle, his mother and father, Yoyok himself, his brother, his sister and even the babysitter in 1974. The other picture was taken 43 years later. The only thing on it that looks completely unchanged is the Beetle.

Yoyok shrugs when they ask him how many kilometres the Beetle now has on the clock. However, it doesn't really matter, anyway. What matters is that the Beetle runs and keeps on running, not only on the road but also through the family. Indonesians often leave their cars to the next generation. In the case of this Beetle: for as many generations as possible. ♥

Model VW Beetle (1200/1500)
Year of manufacture 1962
Location Jakarta
Country Indonesia
Owned by Yoyok Waluyo

Prague / Czech Republic

Unearthing the past

It took sixteen years of research until Ondřej Brom from Prague could be certain: The car in his garage was probably the world's oldest surviving series production Beetle.

The little car which Ondřej Brom had bought in Mariánské Lázně, the former Marienbad, did not exactly make things easy for him. It didn't seem to want to reveal its true identity. However, the Beetle expert was certain of one thing: the body had to be really, really old. It had also definitely been put onto a much younger non-matching chassis. But a VIN plate? A proper, stamped number? Nope. On KdF-Wagens, the typical vehicle identification information was usually stamped onto the inside of the bonnet. However, over the years, the ravages of time and various repair and restoration attempts had eliminated anything that could hint at the original information.

However, there were other signs which told the expert that this had to be a very old Type 60L, despite the numerous small details that had gradually been changed over

Ondřej Brom **did not rest until he had uncovered the true identity of his 1941 Volkswagen Type 60L with the help of the huge international Beetle community. His fellow Beetle enthusiasts gave him tips, spare parts and also shared their knowledge with him.**

the years, such as certain panel shapes and the position of the mounting holes and brackets for the electrics, for example. Ondřej therefore travelled to the veteran VW rally in Bad Camberg in Hesse, Germany, just north of Frankfurt, armed with pictures and everything that he already knew. That is where he met Jacek Krajewski, a walking VW encyclopaedia. He is Polish, one of the best seriously vintage Beetle restorers in the world and was, of course, able to help Ondřej, even though neither of them spoke the other's language. They actually understood each other quite well. "I would ask him something in Czech, and he would answer in Polish," Ondřej says and laughs. Jacek confirmed that the Type 60L was a model that had been produced between 1940 and 1942.

Jacek also gave Ondřej Brom important tips on where else he could look for the information sticker that told the assembly workers at the factory which particular parts they were to fit to this body as the vehicles were basically still assembled more or less manually back then. The range of different specifications was still huge, and the respectively correct bonnets, doors and wings therefore had to be fitted individually.

20. Twenty. A two and a zero. Ondřej Brom found these two digits underneath many layers of paint on the inside of the right-hand side panel. Things progressed rapidly after that, because thanks to the fact that Jacek had been able to tell him roughly when the car was manufactured and the respective literature, he was finally able to work it all out. The vehicle was a KdF-Wagen built in early November 1941 with the chassis number K004292 and the engine number K003913; a

Then and now: **Mariánské Lázně, the former Marienbad, is at the heart of this unusual Beetle story. Antonin Tesar, the son of a previous owner, 67 years ago and today.**

Type 60L, so therefore a saloon with a body that was extremely similar to the prototype from 1939. The vehicle was delivered to Berlin on 5 November 1941. Its first owner: the German operetta composer Paul Lincke. The NS regime had given him the car to mark his 75th birthday.

Paul who? The name Paul Lincke meant as little to Ondřej Brom as it would to most people anywhere in the world – and indeed, even in Germany, Lincke's country of birth – until someone plays a record of the operetta "Frau Luna", maybe, or you hear the hugely popular song "Berliner Luft", Berlin's unofficial anthem, which were both composed by Lincke. Thanks to the internet, Ondřej could hope to learn more about the composer and his Beetle. Paul Lincke had worked at the Marienbad city theatre (in West Bohemia; Marienbad is now known as Mariánské Lázně) as its conductor between 1943 and 1945. So that is how the Beetle came to Marienbad from Berlin, where Lincke had lived previously, but how did the vehicle survive there until Ondřej acquired it?

Now that he knew more, he immediately left Prague for Mariánské Lázně to do some more research. As almost all of the old documents in the city archive are in German, he asked his good friend Jiři, who speaks perfect German, for help. All in all, it took them around a year to find the answers they were looking for. The archive documents included a confiscation notice from the time shortly after the war and even the register entry that recorded a change of ownership. It was dated 1948 – so already written in Czech – and confirmed that someone called Antonin Tesar was the new owner. After a brief search, he found Antonin Tesar. Or rather, his son, who has the same name. He still lives in Mariánské Lázně, as Marienbad has now been called for a long time. Antonin not only had photographs from back then; he was also able to explain many more details to Ondřej. The elderly gentleman remembered, for example, that the entire car was painted light blue, a popular colour in the Eastern Bloc. Ondřej had actually already spotted this "paint job" during his restoration work.

Someone from Germany supplied some more helpful details. Christian Grundmann is the founder of the Rometsch-Museum in Hessisch Oldendorf in Germany, where he exhibits over half a dozen Beetle-based Rometsch classics. He has also managed to reconstruct the 1938 Beetle prototype from fragments, a valiant effort, and is another important expert on very early Volkswagens. Surprisingly, Ondřej's KdF-body still consists of a remarkably high number of original parts. The only thing that did not belong to this Beetle from day one was the chassis. Ondřej has managed to source a KdF chassis that was manufactured around the right time. Lincke's Beetle now rests on this chassis. After an eventful life, it has now found its "forever home" with the Volkswagen fan from Prague. ♥

Thanks for your help:
the fourteen people who helped
Ondřej were each given
a specially designed box with a
dedication and a small piece of
the original panels.

Model Volkswagen Type 60L
Year of manufacture 1941
Location Prague
Country Czech Republic
Owned by Ondřej Brom

T

Trondheim / Norway

Silver shadows

Øystein is a pretty cool guy. He is always dressed stylishly casual and wears a rakish flat cap, too. The Norwegian spent a long time searching for his perfect car. His dream: something with the essence of the Hebmüller convertible and the zest of a Stoll coupe. The result: the Wiger coupe. Thomas Torjesen helped him to interpret and realise his dream.

This is a story about long distances and the wide, wide world. For a start, Norway is a long distance away from Wolfsburg, and Øystein Asphjell and Thomas Torjesen are even further away from each other – or they were back when they started an unusual Beetle project together, even though they are actually both Norwegians. Thomas lived in the USA for many years, where he made a name for himself on the custom scene as a member of Salinas Boys Customs. This place, around 180 kilometres to the south of San Francisco, is one of the most famous customs specialists on the US custom car scene. Øystein, for his part, studied for a while in Austin/Texas, which is how he heard of what the Salinas Boys were all about: "Clean and Low".

Thomas returned to Norway a few years ago and set up Norwegian Hammerworks in Fredrikstad, which lies to the south

of Oslo, so essentially as far south as you can go in Norway, in an attempt to recreate the feeling of the custom car scene in the southern states of the USA. Perfect timing, as Øystein thought that Thomas could be the one to realise and fine-tune his car dreams. His fantastic idea was already almost set in stone: he wanted to create a previously non-existent symbiosis between the legendary Hebmüller convertible and the so-called Stoll coupe – only even more beautiful, and definitely totally unique. One-off, customised cars were actually not that rare up until the 1950s. "Couturiers", as the countless coachbuilding companies called themselves back then, turned existing vehicles into unique customised versions, always to the customer's specifications – provided they were technically feasible.

Øystein was inspired to attempt this project when he heard of the Stoll coupe for the first time. In 1952, the coachbuilding company Stoll from Bad Nauheim in Hesse, Germany, converted an Export model from a classic four-seater into a sleek coupe for a lawyer. They modelled the conversion on the so-called Hebmüller convertible manufactured in Wülfrath near Wuppertal, also in Germany. Hebmüller had recently been forced to file for insolvency due to a major fire in May 1952. Several banks had refused to give the company a loan – despite the fact that its order books were full.

Typical for the Hebmüller model was an elongated front bonnet, which Øystein definitely also wanted on his version because he preferred it to the one on the Stoll coupe, which he modelled his custom Beetle on and which is still on display at the VW Museum in Wolfsburg. He therefore wanted the silhouette to be similar to the outline

Øystein Asphjell (on the left) has an extremely individual taste in Beetles. He realised his dream Beetle together with Thomas Torjesen. The result is a coupe so meticulously crafted that painting it would only distract from the craftsmanship.

PHOTOS STEFAN BAU   TEXT KLAUS MORHAMMER

Unique from every angle. **A crotch cooler Beetle has been turned into a unique custom car that is an homage to the American hardtop coupes of the 1940s and 1950s. Truly a dream!**

of the Hebmüller convertible with the roof up. This also meant a small rear window, no rear side windows and only two seats (however, with an extended parcel shelf behind them). Even though Øystein, as an engineer, had technical know-how and skills, he was glad that he was able to realise the project together with Thomas from Norwegian Hammerworks. Thomas agreed straight away; he thought it was a phenomenal idea, of course.

It took the two of them seven months to work out the final shape of the coupe roof. After that, they began to look for a base vehicle that was worthy of undergoing this transformation. As is so often the case with projects like this, serendipity helped Øystein to find an almost rust-free imported Beetle still equipped with its original engine – both built in 1952. Granted, the previous owner had fitted rectangular windows from a 1958 model, but they were going to take the roof off, anyway. The question of how to design the area where the new roof edge meets the windscreen frame was more complex. On the original Hebmüller, this part looks pretty much like the bony forehead of Neanderthal man, rather than meticulous precision work. A window frame from a 1954 cabriolet turned up, again

serendipitously, and fitted beautifully into Øystein's dream. However, when it came to the rear window, they decided to use a made-to-measure version that looks the same as the convertible windows of the time but is less curved which, according to the creators, gives the car a considerably more well-balanced overall look. All that remained was the question of how to design the area where the coupe roof meets the body at the rear. The skills of the Norwegian Hammerworks owner again saved the day. Perfectly shaped curves, produced on the basis of templates copied from the Hebmüller convertible with the roof up, not only fulfil their purpose but also look outrageously good. They continued with the front door corners, which curve gently upwards, like on the Hebmüller. The two also applied their perfectionism to the semaphore indicator recesses. They are no longer located on the front side panels, like they were on the Hebmüller. Instead, they have been beautifully integrated into the B pillar extensions where, for space reasons, they were also located on convertibles since the days of the 1951/52 crotch cooler Beetles.

To give their audience the chance to fully appreciate the outstanding craftsmanship that has gone into Øystein's creation, its two creators agreed to use only clear lacquer on the bodywork, for the time being. The idea was that it will get an exquisite original paint job later on. They wanted to show off their handiwork at a major rally first to prove their point. The interior was also still in an unrestored but nevertheless reasonable condition. It looks what you would expect the interior of a Hebmüller from this decade to look like. However, this model is something really special: a genuine Wiger coupe. The name was inspired by Øystein's grandfather; the coupe is dedicated to him. However, that's another story about another pretty cool guy.

♥

Model VW custom conversion, "Wiger" coupe
Year of manufacture 1952 (base vehicle)
Location Trondheim
Country Norway
Owned by Øystein Asphjell

C

Laughing children, ancient walls: These Beetles have found an idyllic home in Chartres.

L'amour toujours

Alexandre succumbed to the charms of a Beetle made in Mexico as a student. As a recently qualified doctor, the young Frenchman fulfilled himself his dream of owning a split rear window Beetle – manufactured in 1950 – and a few years later, he also bought himself his second dream Beetle, a 1951 convertible. Completely different stories link him to both cars. He loves his Beetles, and intends to go on adding to his small collection.

Teheran airport, summer 1998. Nervously, a French national puts his luggage on the conveyor belt. The metal parts in his suitcase could cause some difficulties, to put it mildly. Luckily, all of the luggage belonging to the young medical student with Iranian roots passed the scanner without causing a major uproar. These treasures – cylinder heads for a 1950 Beetle – would allow Alexandre Arash Djavadian to continue to restore his split rear window Beetle.

He had already caught the "Bug bug" as a very young man. First clear "symptom": a 1985 Beetle made in Mexico. "My first own car had to be cheap, easy to repair and also eye-catching. A Beetle was the obvious answer. At some point, I wanted to drive a proper classic Beetle," the now 44-year-old recalls. "So I bought myself a split rear window model in 1997. The car was offered for sale in a Belgian newspaper advertisement. It was in a

terrible condition," Alex says, remembering that day. Almost 50 years after Mademoiselle Plaineveau had ordered the pastel-green Bug on 17 May 1950, her daughter still found it difficult to part with the car of her childhood. However, when she talked to Alex, she realised that the future doctor would treat the car well. They agreed the sale over Belgian waffles and cake. The Beetle needed a lot of work.

A year after he had bought the car, a visit to the provinces of Lower Saxony in Germany turned out to be very fortunate indeed for Alex. To this day, Beetle fans regularly hold a rally in the small town of Hessisch Oldendorf, where the Grundmann family lives. "I told Christian Grundmann that I would love to take part in the pageant but didn't have a car," Alex recalls; at this point, the Belgian Mademoiselle's Beetle was still in anything but a good condition. All of a sudden, he found himself sitting in a convertible driven by Bernd Heimbold from Hameln. "One of us – that was me – spoke no German, and the other no French," says Alex about their first meeting and laughs. This meeting led to a friendship that lasts to this day, as Bernd borrowed Alex the exact same convertible for his wedding when he got married in 2000, "...because your Beetle isn't finished yet and you need a decent wedding car," Bernd stated categorically. There was more: "Bernd and Christian helped me to finish the Beetle during the most stressful periods of my student days," Alex says, appreciating the efforts his German friends put into the car.

Thanks to many helping hands, it was finally finished in 2014. After seventeen years of work, the saloon now looks as good as new. "Spending time with my second family, my VW friends, means a lot to me.

Alexandre Arash Djavadian is a doctor who also likes to visit his patients in one of his two split rear window Beetles from time to time

Through narrow alleyways onto light-filled squares: Alex's Beetles shine almost as brightly as the sun.

Vintage accessories and matching details complete the authentic look of this largely original convertible Beetle; the suitcases are always on board, just in case...

What is so special about them is the warmth and sense of community," Alex says in an attempt to describe his feelings. At one of the many meetings with his fellow enthusiasts, whilst his Beetle from Belgium was actually still in the middle of being restored, Alex mentioned that his ultimate dream would be a classic Beetle in original condition that had never been touched before. "If I could find a classic model like that, it would have to be a 1951 convertible," the Frenchman joked at the time. One of his VW friends, convertible expert Claus Missing, cleared his throat and said that around ten years previously, someone had offered him a convertible Beetle at a classic car show. Only one owner, built in 1951. Supposedly all original. The body and the floorpan had never been apart.

Back then, he thought the offer was too good to be true; however, Claus still followed it up. The seller persisted with his story: the car was as described but as good as sold. A few weeks later, the man contacted Missing again: if he was still interested in the car, he could come and have a look at it. The potential buyer was unable to proceed with the purchase as he suddenly found himself behind bars. A wild story. However, one with a happy end. Claus bought the car and passed it on

to Alex after a major barter transaction. That is how Alex acquired the convertible – which was built and delivered to a Hans Weber in Germany's Allgäu region on 6 July 1951 – as a sort of automotive "amuse bouche" during his folding roof Beetle restoration project.

The convertible turned out to be a lucky find, after all. It had been driven by its first owner until the 1990s and had been serviced regularly by the local VW dealer, as proven by lots of invoices and receipts and a pair of old metal-rimmed spectacles. "I found them underneath the passenger seat. His leather gloves were also still in the car. I've never seen all of these accessories still together in the same place," he says proudly.

Whilst Alex admires his VW treasures on the dining table of his apartment in a beautiful period building, his family returns home. Ever since he left medical school in Paris, Alex has lived in the picturesque historic city centre of Chartres, which lies to the south-west of the busy French capital, with his wife Alexandra and their two daughters Apolline and Astrid. They share their father's love for old Volkswagens and enjoy helping him with some of the smaller jobs to make sure that when the weather is nice, papa can also do his rounds in the "Cox", which is short for Coccinelle, the French for beetle. The general practitioner can't answer the question of which of his two Beetles is his favourite. On the one side, there is the folding roof Beetle lovingly restored over many years and on the other, the well-maintained convertible with its original roof, original seats and the original 25 bhp engine. Indeed, a difficult choice to make. "Actually, I would like to start to look for a 1954 standard Beetle and the respective spare parts all over the world," Alex says, laughing. A serious sounding harrumph can be heard from the kitchen... ♥

Model "Export" model with split rear window
and folding roof (Type 117)
Year of manufacture 1950
Location Chartres
Country France
Owned by Dr Alexandre
Arash Djavadian

Model Split rear window
convertible (Type 151)
Year of manufacture 1951
Location Chartres
Country France
Owned by Dr Alexandre
Arash Djavadian

Safely united under one roof: a Beetle duo in place of the busy market stalls.

Endless skies, endless countryside. Let's go!

From father to son, from a moment to eternity. On the road forever!

We would like to thank everyone who believed in this book. First and foremost, though, the enthusiasts all over the world who shared their treasures, and sometimes their life stories, with us. One thing they all have in common is Volkswagens. A huge community whose members meet wherever they can: at rallies, in online forums – or simply driving along. Regardless of whether they are rich or poor, which language they speak or which religion they follow, or whether they are young or old: none of these things matter. The only important thing is their shared love for Beetles.

German National Library bibliographic information
This publication has been recorded by the German National Library in the Deutsche Nationalbibliografie index of all publications issued in Germany; the bibliographic details are available online at http://dnb.dnb.de.

1st edition
ISBN 978-3-667-11390-0
© Delius, Klasing & Co. KG, Bielefeld

Concept: Edwin Baaske, Dr Nadja Kneissler
Publisher: Thorsten Elbrigmann
Editors: Michael Blumenstein, Klaus Morhammer, Angela Tegtmeier, Heiko P. Wacker

Authors: Ingo Eiberg, Thorsten Elbrigmann, Bastian Fuhrmann, Tina Gallach, Thomas Imhoff, Eberhard Kittler, Michael Kneissler, Klaus Morhammer, Petronella Nicholson, Christina Rahmes, Magdalena Rutschmann-Weinle, Dokke Sahertian, Martin Santoro, Wolfgang Schäffer, Lena Siep, Stacy Suaya, Heiko P. Wacker

Photographers: Tim Adler, Theodor Barth, Stefan Bau, Christian Blanck, Markus Bolsinger, Jan Bürgermeister, James Davison, Thorsten Doerk, Hartmut Elbrigmann, Inge Feltrinelli (Fotogloria), Götz Göppert, Patrick Gosling, Ivan und Beth Hodges, Dominikus and Zainab Hocher, Anatol Kotte, Andreas Lindlahr, Stephan Lindloff, Lisa Linke, Michael Papendieck, Stephan Repke, Dokke Sahertian, Misha Vallejo, Volkswagen Archive

Copy editor: Petra Schomburg
Translation: Paulina Nowak, Sprachenfabrik GmbH
Art director: Jörg Weusthoff
Cover design and layout: Weusthoff Noël, Hamburg
Cover photograph: Johannes Höhn
Production manager: Axel Gerber and Jörn Heese
Colour printing: Mohn Media, Gütersloh
Printed by: Kunst- und Werbedruck, Bad Oeynhausen
Printed in Germany 2018

Delius Klasing Verlag, Siekerwall 21, 33602 Bielefeld, Germany
Phone: +49 521/559-0, fax: +49 521/559-115
Email: info@delius-klasing.de
www.delius-klasing.de